Carrickfergus, Whitehead and the Great War.

'across the hawthorn hedge the noise of bugles...'

(from *Carrickfergus* by Louis McNeice, 1937)

Foreward

The Mid-Antrim Museums Service has attempted over the years to reveal local stories that have too long been buried inside the larger narrative of Ireland's participation in the Great War. Exhibitions in Ballymena, Carrickfergus and Larne museums and community history projects delivered through the Service have enabled local people to learn more about how the war affected their families and their neighbourhoods.

Another significant project developed with Newtownabbey Museum Service, involved the publication of a book about the life and death of Tom McKinney of Sentry Hill, drawing on a family archive of letters and photographs which have survived from that era.

Philip Orr's book about Tom McKinney painted a picture of how the war deeply affected an individual farming family from that part of County Antrim. With this new book, Philip turns his attention to the impact made by the conflict on another nearby part of the county, and to the tragic consequences for so many local families in Carrickfergus and Whitehead who lost loved ones in a war whose reverberations can still be felt today.

Jayne Clarke
Curator
Mid-Antrim Museums Service

Introduction

The huge growth of interest in Ireland's experience of the Great War has been a remarkable feature of the last twenty years of local history. There are numerous books about Irish soldiers and Irish regiments. There has been a renewed desire to commemorate the dead and to visit the battlefields and the graveyards where they were buried. The story of Ireland's experience of the Great War has tended understandably to focus on the horrors of trench warfare, and the huge and wasteful battles in which so many local soldiers participated. However there is also an interesting story to tell about how the war impacted on everyday domestic life, in a country that was teetering on the brink of civil conflict in 1914 and would enter a period of intense political strife soon after the Great War ended in 1918.

One of the best ways to do justice to the domestic story is to follow the course of the war within one small region. The location on which this book focuses is the northern shoreline of Belfast Lough and in particular, the towns of Carrickfergus and Whitehead and their coastal hinterlands. Through studying the regional newspapers, the photographs, the autobiographical writings and the letters that have survived from that era, it is possible to draw a fascinating picture of how local people experienced life in wartime.

A close look at these two towns during the war-years offers many insights. Carrickfergus was a long-established settlement and it had seen military activity in every century since medieval times. By contrast, Whitehead was largely a product of the Victorian period and it had become a highly popular 'leisure destination' for the middle classes by 1914. Both towns existed in a part of Ireland with strong maritime traditions. The reader of this book should thus be able to sense the impact of the war on Irish coastal communities, on ports, on barracks towns and on seaside resorts. The reader will also have a chance to observe the impact of the war on a small, regional population that possessed – as it still does – a very large Protestant majority.

As the historical account of the Great War period in Ireland becomes clearer and more detailed and more aware of subtle regional differences, there are real benefits which can accrue. The present generation may become less prone to making the unguarded generalisations which lie at the heart of historical myth-making. They may become better equipped to understand the twelve years of complex political conflict from 1911 to 1922 within its global context of imperial rivalry and fracture, intense ideological contest and worldwide national resurgence.

This is a period which shaped all of our destinies on this island. In understanding it more fully we enhance our capacity to deal judiciously with our varied present-day allegiances and increase our ability to shape shared and peaceful communities, free from the blight of war.

Philip Orr, January 2010

Philip Orr is a writer, researcher and educationalist whose work on the Great War includes The Road to The Somme (1987, 2008); Field of Bones (2006) and Tom's Story (2007).

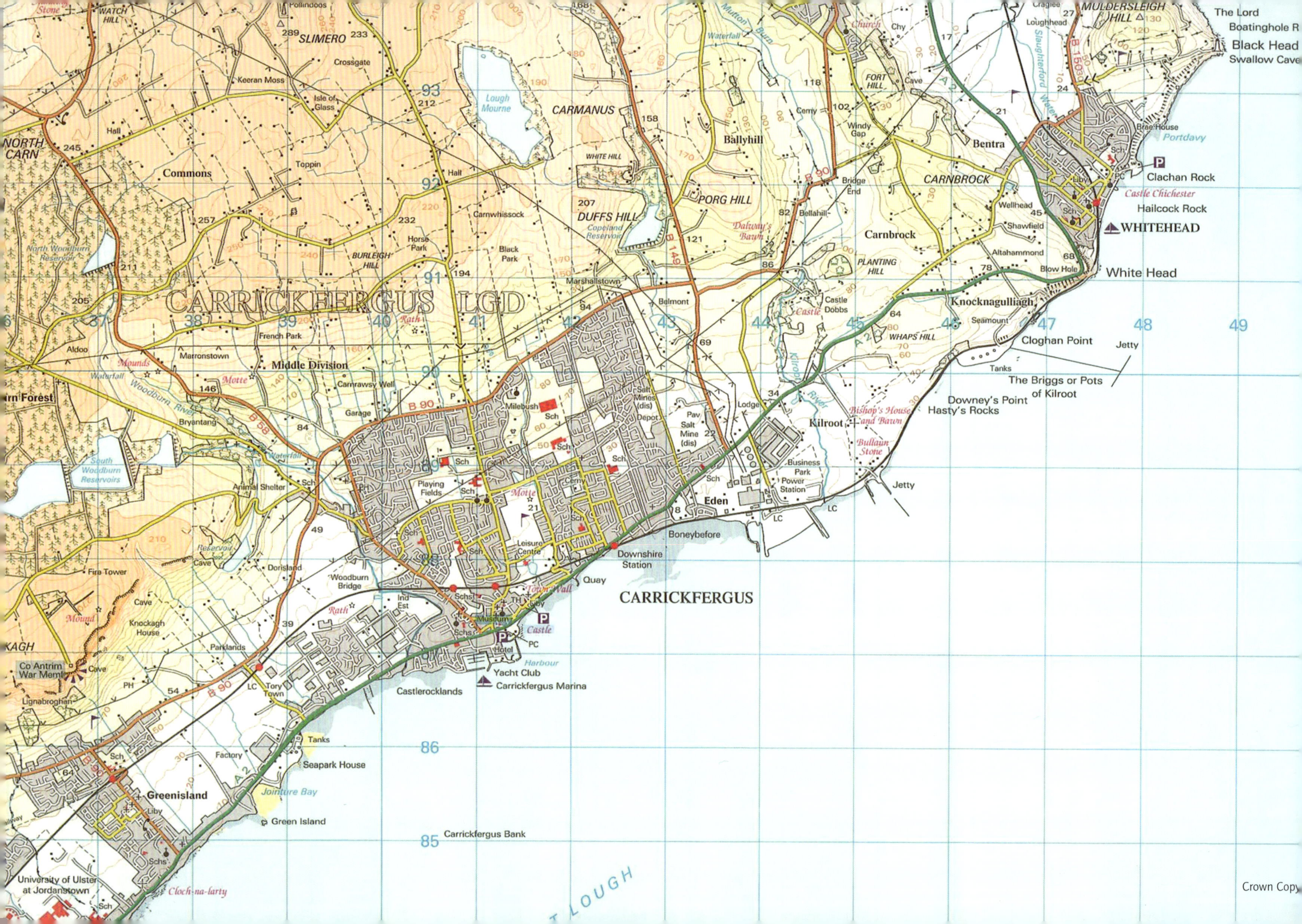

CARRICKFERGUS LGD
CARRICKFERGUS
WHITEHEAD
White Head
Black Head
Swallow Cave
The Lord
Boatinghole R
MULDERSLEIGH HILL
Loughhead
Portdavy
Brae House
Clachan Rock
Castle Chichester
Hailcock Rock
Blow Hole
Knocknagulliagh
Seamount
Cloghan Point
Jetty
Tanks
The Briggs or Pots of Kilroot
Downey's Point
Hasty's Rocks
Kilroot
Bishop's House and Bawn
Bullaun Stone
Business Park
Power Station
Eden
Boneybefore
Downshire Station
Quay
Castle
Harbour
Yacht Club
Carrickfergus Marina
Castlerocklands
Tanks
Seapark House
Jointure Bay
Green Island
Greenisland
Carrickfergus Bank
University of Ulster at Jordanstown
Cloch-na-larty
LOUGH
Crown Copy
SLIMERO
Crossgate
Keeran Moss
Isle of Glass
Lough Mourne
CARMANUS
WHITE HILL
DUFFS HILL
Copeland Reservoir
PORG HILL
Ballyhill
Windy Gap
FORT HILL
Bentra
CARNBROCK
Carnbrock
Wellhead
Shawfield
Altahammond
PLANTING HILL
Castle Dobbs
WHAPS HILL
Belmont
Marshallstown
Dalway's Bawn
Bellahill
Bridge End
Commons
Toppin
Carnwhissock
Horse Park
Black Park
BURLEIGH HILL
NORTH CARN
North Woodburn Reservoir
French Park
Middle Division
Marronstown
Aldoo
Mounds
Motte
Waterfall
Woodburn River
Bryantang
Carnrawsy Well
Milebush
Salt Mines (dis)
Salt Mine (dis)
Depot
Lodge
Kilroot River
South Woodburn Reservoirs
Animal Shelter
Playing Fields
Leisure Centre
Town Wall
Museum
Hotel
Dorisland
Woodburn Bridge
Ind Est
Rath
Fire Tower
Knockagh House
Parklands
Co Antrim War Meml
Lignabroghan
Tory Town
Factory
B 90
B 58
B 149
A 2
37
38
39
40
41
42
43
44
45
46
47
48
49
93
92
91
90
89
88
86
85

Prelude

On the eve of the Great War, Carrickfergus was the most important settlement on the northern shores of Belfast Lough. When the 1911 national census was taken, the town possessed 4,300 inhabitants, while another 1,200 people lived in the rural environment immediately to the south-west of the town, on the way towards Belfast. To the north-east of Carrickfergus, a population of 2,500 lived within a short distance of the lough-shore. They included the 1,300 inhabitants of the elegant seaside resort of Whitehead, which lay between two scenic headlands. The population of Whitehead doubled during the summer season and owed its seasonal growth to the efficient County Antrim railway network.

The people of Carrickfergus were conscious of living in an historic town, dominated by a strong and impressive Anglo-Norman castle. However they were well aware that during the 18th and 19th centuries, their town had been overtaken in importance by Belfast, which was situated just twelve miles away. By 1914 Belfast was an industrial city of global importance.

Industry did exist in Carrickfergus but on a much smaller scale. There was salt-mining, flax-spinning, weaving, bleaching and printing. Ship-building and commercial fishing had once been important but both activities had virtually ceased by the 1900s. The ancient harbour still did business, enhanced by a recently erected pier. It exported local salt and it imported coal and military supplies. Carrickfergus was a railway town on the route to Larne, where a cross-channel ferry operated. Whitehead's railway station was also a thronged place in the summer months. Visitors came to stay in the town's hotels or villas. They frequented its tea-houses, walked along its promenade or bathed on the shore.

Carrickfergus was a barracks town, home to a unit of the Royal Garrison Artillery. It possessed an ordnance depot and was the location for a recently opened infantry camp at Sunnylands on the North Road. It was also the

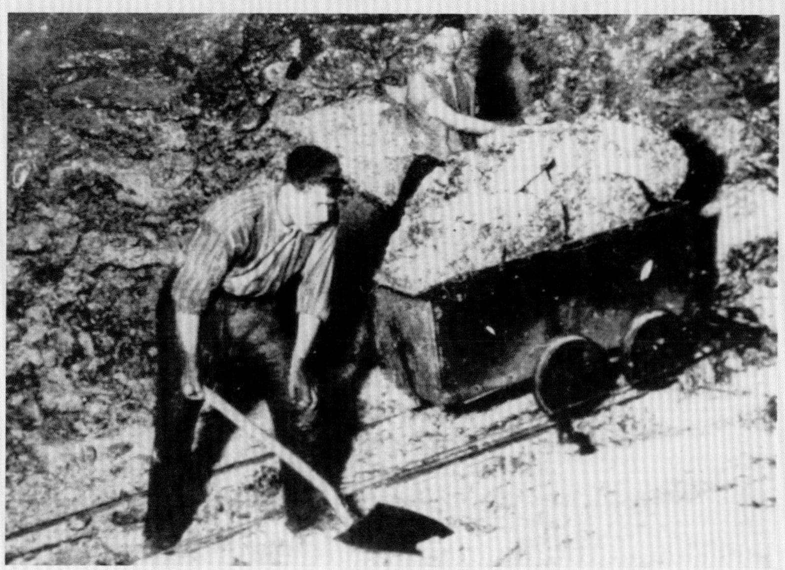

2

1. The northern shoreline of Belfast Lough today.
2. Salt-miners at Kilroot.

childhood home of the poet Louis MacNeice. His father was rector of St. Nicholas' Church of Ireland. This ancient building had a cruciform structure and possessed distinctive sculptures commemorating the Chichester family who had presided over the walled town of Carrickfergus in the early 17th century, when English settlers were beginning to exercise dominance over the old Gaelic kingdoms of Ulster. Young Louis was intrigued by the nave in his father's church, built at an angle to the horizontal, in order to mirror the 'list' of Christ's head as he hung on the cross.

In later writings about his childhood, MacNeice gave a vivid portrait of his home town during the years just before and during the Great War. The young boy relished the view of 'the wrinkled lough' and he adored the green rectory garden, which was 'a long prairie of lawn and virgin shrubberies'. He admired the sturdy castle walls and the prosperous seafront houses which stood along the Scotch Quarter but he observed with trepidation the poverty and ill-health in the damp, candle-lit houses of the Irish Quarter where men stood 'with cloth caps pulled down over narrow leering eyes' and the pavements were 'constellated with spit'.

The young boy noted the evidence of Ulster's stark religious enmities and saw 'drab cement walls' where the words 'to hell with the pope' were chalked up. He was growing up in a part of Ulster which possessed only a small Catholic population. In rural areas of south-east Antrim, Catholics rarely exceeded 5% of the population, although in Carrickfergus itself, that figure rose to nearly 12%. Catholics lived as a minority in almost every part of the town but only three of the town's 32 thoroughfares possessed no Catholic residents, during the 1911 census.

Louis MacNeice's autobiographical writings reveal how as a child he heard the typical sounds of a small, maritime, industrial town, situated close to the Ulster countryside - 'fog-horn, mill-horn, corncrake and church bell.' And as the rectory was close to Sunnylands camp, he also heard 'across the hawthorn hedge the noise of bugles.' This was the daily ritual of Last Post and Reveille, being sounded in Carrickfergus in time-honoured military fashion. Europe was about to be convulsed by war but most inhabitants of Carrickfergus and Whitehead would have felt that they were situated a long way off from the potential battlefields, living on the shores of an Irish sea-lough, on the western edge of the continent. However the area was to be deeply affected by the Great War, a conflict more costly and more global than anything yet witnessed in history.

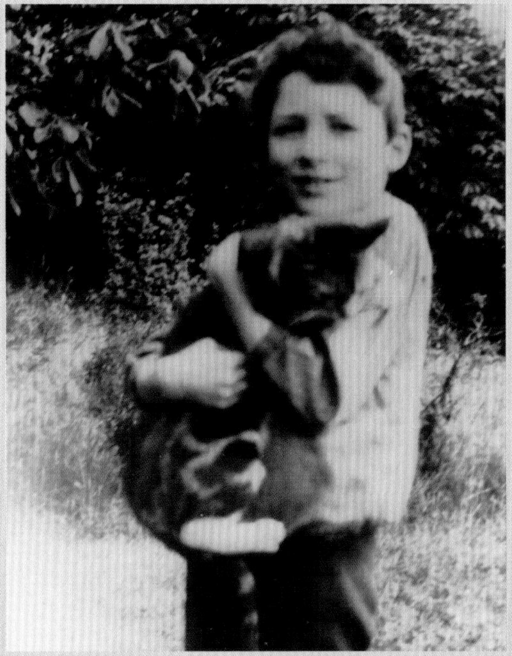
3

3. The young Louis MacNeice in the St Nicholas rectory garden.

1914

Early in 1914, attention in Carrickfergus and Whitehead was focused on Irish politics, not on wider European affairs. A Home Rule Bill was passing through parliament in Westminster, giving Ireland a government of its own in Dublin and a measure of independence inside the British Empire. A public campaign, which was centred in Ulster, opposed this legislation. The campaign was rooted in fear that the Protestants who predominated in north-eastern Ireland would become an underprivileged minority in an autonomous Ireland, dominated by poverty and Catholicism.

In September 1912, bonfires blazed on Whitehead's seafront to celebrate the signing of the document known as the Ulster Covenant, in which hundreds of thousands of citizens vowed to resist Home Rule. The Carrickfergus streets were decorated with Union Jacks and bunting. When an Ulster Volunteer Force was formed in order to oppose Home Rule with force, many men enrolled in it. They became members of No 3 battalion of the local UVF regiment. These Ulster Volunteers assembled on such open spaces as the Whitehead esplanade and the sports ground near the Barn Mills in Carrickfergus. By 1914 they had learned to drill, to march and to carry dummy weapons. The Whitehead men carried out exercises on the golf course, to the bemusement of English and Scottish holiday-makers, who were a regular feature of the summer season.

Before long, an Irish National Volunteer movement had been formed amongst nationalists, to back up the Home Rule cause with arms. In March, Carrickfergus became aware of just how seriously the British government was taking the threat of civil war in Ireland, when they witnessed the arrival of 250 men from the Kings Own Yorkshire Light Infantry, who occupied Sunnylands camp. These troops were deployed to remind the Ulster Volunteer Force that Irish Home Rule was government policy and to act as 'peacekeepers' should clashes materialize between the rival Irish militias. The Yorkshiremen arrived by cruiser in March 1914 and disembarked at Carrickfergus harbour.

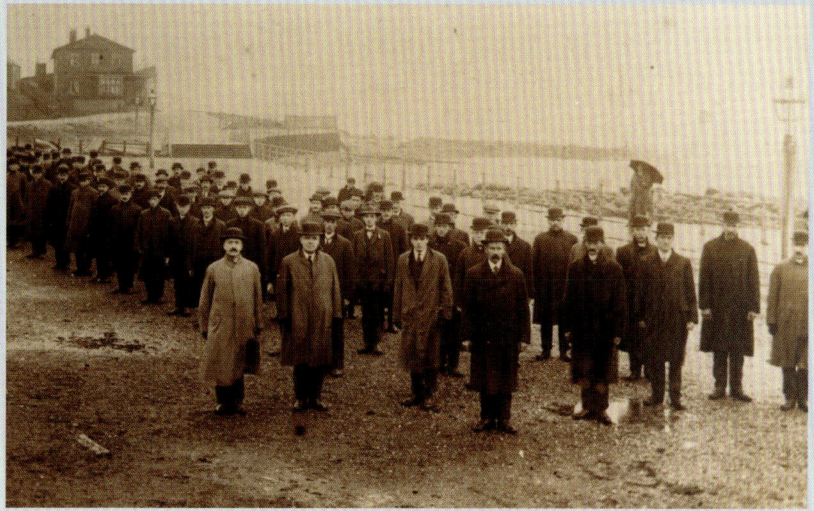

4

4. An early photograph of the Ulster Volunteer Force at Whitehead.

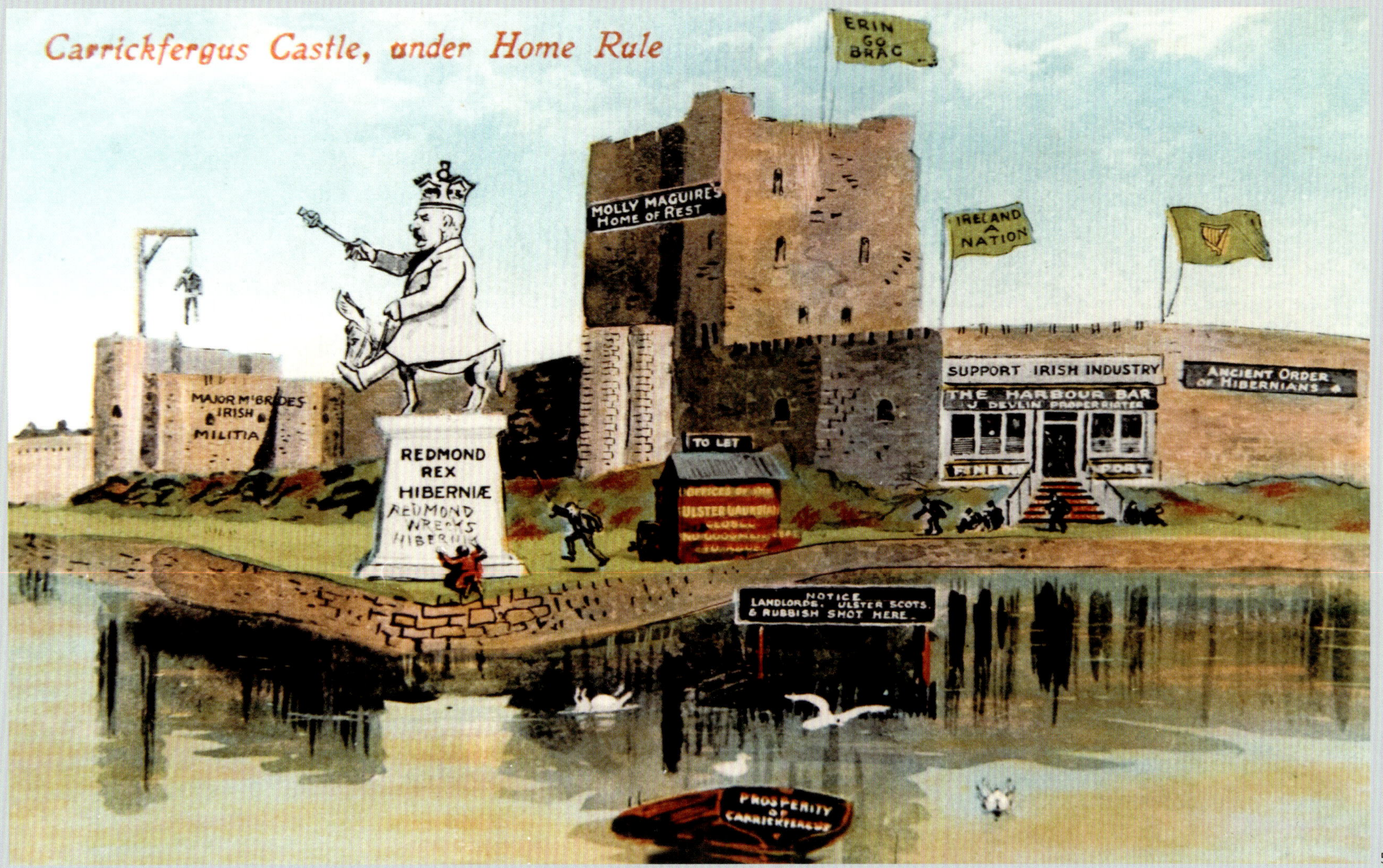

5

5. A local Anti-Home Rule Postcard.

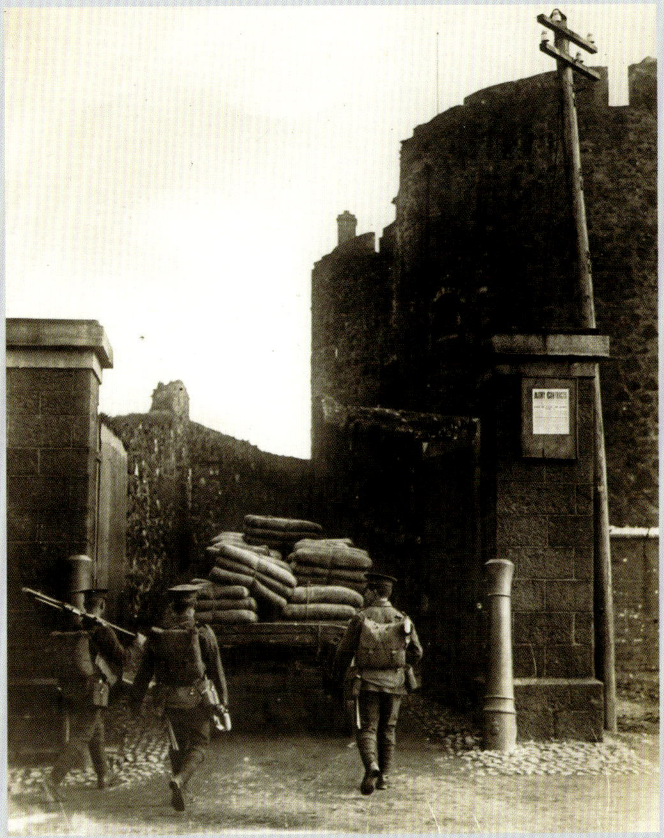

6

6. English soldiers arrive at Carrickfergus during the Home Rule Crisis.

The Ulster Volunteers were not the only local militants. Emulating similar outrages in England, a group of suffragettes had recently exploded small bombs in Ulster and they had set fire to several 'big houses', including a mansion overlooking the sea at Whiteabbey and another at Orlands, to the north-east of Carrickfergus.

Such issues were soon overshadowed. In July, Irish newspapers carried the story of an assassination in the Bosnian town of Sarajevo, inside the Austro-Hungarian Empire. The Austrian Archduke had been killed by revolutionaries who wanted to transfer Bosnian allegiance to the adjacent nation of Serbia. Soon Austria had declared war on Serbia. Before long Serbia's ally, Russia, had been drawn into conflict, as had Austria, which was a friend of Germany. Fearing an early attack from France – which was allied to Russia - Germany mobilized its army to pour through Belgium and head for Paris, before turning to face the Russians. Long-term rivalry between the 'Big Powers' of Europe had boiled over into military conflict.

Britain had signed treaties of friendship with the French and the Belgians and it was the most powerful empire in the world. It could not stand by as German infantry moved steadily towards the English Channel. The citizens of Ulster now faced both a local political crisis and a European war. The tense environment became obvious on 22nd July. The public were banned from Carrickfergus pier, while military ordnance was landed at the harbour, bound for the army stores in High Street. On 4th August, Britain declared war on Germany.

Four years of bloodshed were about to begin.

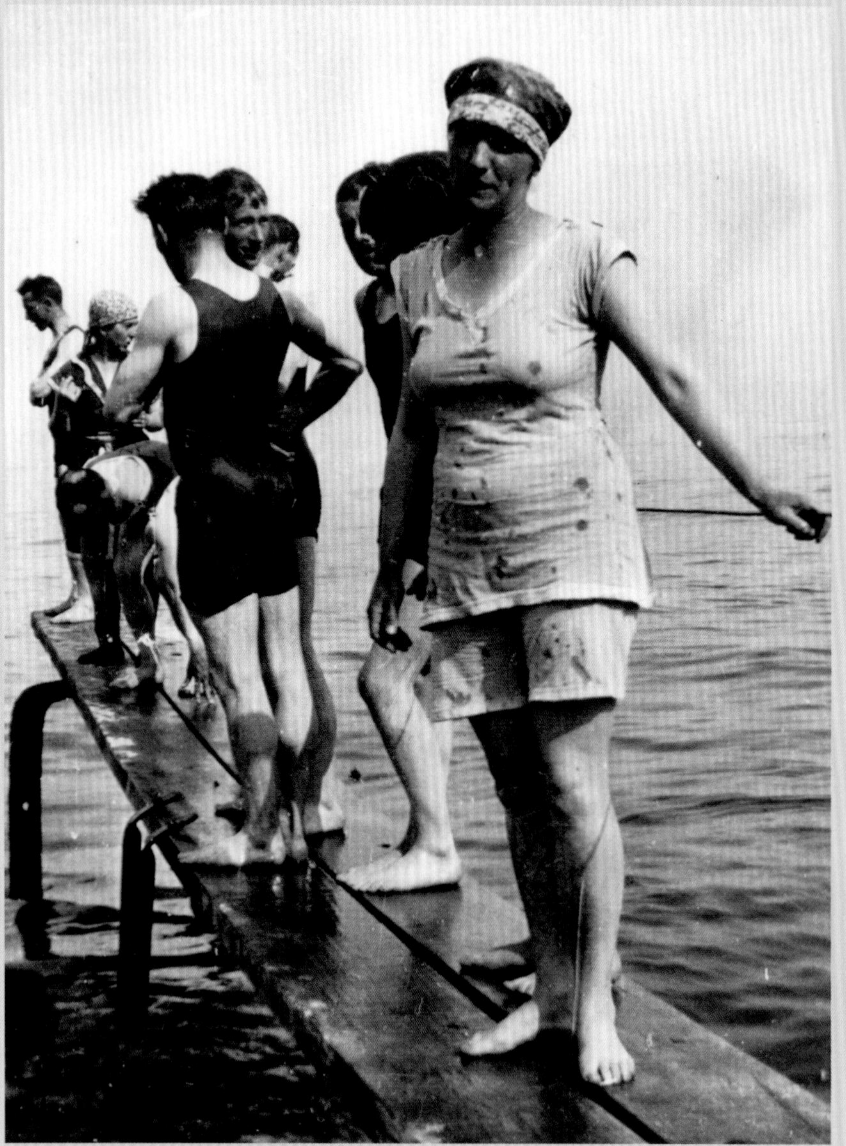

7

7. Bathers at Whitehead, August 1914.

Few locals could have realized the gravity of what lay ahead. Groups of bathers still dived and swam by the rocks near Whitehead railway tunnel, oblivious to the gathering war-clouds. Holiday-makers still strolled along the Esplanade in the pleasant summer weather. Nonetheless, some people probably wondered if they would witness again the famous concerts given in Whitehead by a Viennese band, led by their conductor, Herr Jacobs. Austria, as an ally of Germany, was now an enemy.

Before August was over, there was evidence along the County Antrim coast that war had commenced. The cross-channel cable station at Whitehead was placed under guard. Sentries were posted on the railway-line, at such important locations as the tunnel underneath the cliffs, near where the Whitehead bathing parties had gathered. The boom of artillery was heard from the coastal defence battery at Kilroot and from across Belfast Lough at a similar battery located in Greypoint Fort, where gunners were practising their fire. Meanwhile transport steamers sailed down the lough, taking reserve troops to England and thence to France. Innocent boating came to an end as yachtsmen were forbidden to sail. Cowls were placed on all seaward-facing lights, close to the water's edge.

One of the first regiments of the British Army to encounter the foe in 1914 was the Kings Own Yorkshire Light Infantry, some of whose men had recently served in Ulster. By September, reports of Yorkshire fatalities were circulating. In a memorial service in St Nicholas Church for Yorkshiremen who had died, the rector referred to 'two of the officers killed in the recent fighting near the French frontier', who 'used to occupy a pew near the pulpit' during Sunday worship. Despite the fact that these English soldiers had been sent to quell the Ulster Volunteers, local people had obviously taken at least some of the men to their hearts.

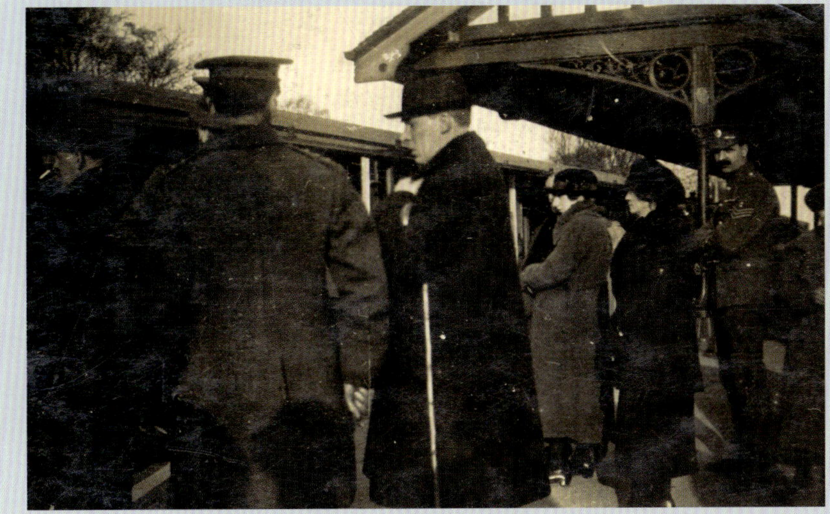
8

The rector of St. Nicholas went on to preach each Sunday throughout the war years, prompting his son in later years to recollect his childish perceptions –

'My father made the walls resound,
He wore his collar the wrong way round....'

In Carrickfergus Museum, Reverend F. J. MacNeice's Bible still exists, as do printed copies of his wartime sermons. Young Louis would eventually refer to his father as

'...courteous
And lyrical and strong and kind and truthful,
A generous puritan....'

In the pre-war months he had refused to sign the Ulster Covenant, seeing at as a divisive gesture and a recipe for even greater civil conflict. In the war years, he had to summon up strength to bring solace to local bereaved families but also to offer nurture to Louis and his two siblings, after the death of their mother in 1914.

Many units of Britain's small pre-war professional army were now in conflict with the Germans. They included Carrickfergus men who had already been in the forces when war was declared. However Britain's main fighting force in recent times had been the navy and its infantry was much too small to help the French tackle the huge German war-machine. The War Secretary, Lord Kitchener, realised that a new mass-army of civilians was required. Across the British Isles, recruitment began. By September, arrangements for implementing Irish Home Rule had been 'frozen' until after the war and an opportunity was given for both the Ulster Volunteer Force and the Irish National Volunteers to offer their military services. Each side lived in hope of favorable treatment from the British government at a later stage. So both unionist and nationalist recruits joined the British Armed Forces, as did many men who possessed no particular political motivation but wished to experience the comradeship and adventure that the army now seemed to offer.

Soon, men from the Ulster Volunteer Force were presenting themselves for soldiering. 120 volunteers from the local UVF battalion queued outside the Barn National School in Scotch Quarter. The first volunteer to step into the building was a man called William Evans. Soon he and his fellow volunteers were undergoing medical examination, to see if they were fit for enrolment. Then those who were of legitimate age and who possessed good health were

8. The rector of St. Nicholas, Reverend MacNeice, watches as troops depart from Carrickfergus Station.

sent to Clandeboye camp in County Down. There they began life as soldiers in the 12th (Mid-Antrim) battalion of the regiment known as the Royal Irish Rifles, within a larger unit known as the 36th (Ulster) Division. This division aimed to recruit 17,000 soldiers, relying for the most part on men from the Ulster Volunteer Force.

Of course, UVF men were not the only locals to join the army. Although it is hard to estimate how many men from a Catholic background volunteered for service, it may be presumed that patterns which existed elsewhere in Ulster were also found here. Recruitment in urban areas of north-eastern Ireland during 1914 tended to be fairly brisk among both Catholics and Protestants. In towns with a 'barracks' tradition, such as Carrickfergus, a number of young, unskilled Catholics would already have found their way into the army as a means of earning a living in the pre-war years.

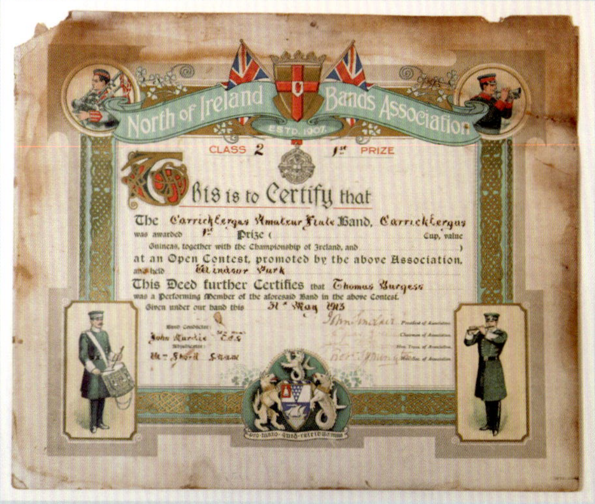

9

9. A local flute band often played when troops marched into or out of Carrickfergus.

Local factories provided numerous recruits. In the Barn Mills, on Taylor's Avenue, volunteers included factory managers such as Archibald Lemon and also men from the shop floor. One employee who joined up was Robbie McAuley, whose pastime was cycling. He entered the Cyclist's Company in the Ulster Division, making friends with a Derry man, George Lindsay. Another employee, Samuel Hill, went with most of his colleagues into the 12th Royal Irish Rifles, leaving his role as a player in the Barn Swifts football team.

The local paper described the scenes as the local UVF men left for the camp at the Clandeboye estate, which was situated near Newtownards –

'The departure of the men yesterday morning was a noteworthy event...they marched through the town, headed by Carrickfergus Amateur Flute Band, and made for the railway station. Along the route there was a lavish display of flags and bunting...the mill lassies were out in great force and added much to the liveliness of the scene with their choruses and cheers...the railway station could scarcely accommodate the throng. As the train steamed into the platform at a quarter past nine, the Larne Volunteers, who occupied the fore part of it, announced their arrival by a lusty cheer, responded to by the occupants of the platform...'

The newspaper displayed a list of 102 men who had passed the medical, convinced the recruiting officer that they were at least 19 years of age and had thus been incorporated into 'Carson's Army.' The 36th Division was thus named by Ulster unionists, in reference to their leader, Sir Edward Carson. Men who were reasonably fit would have had no problem gaining a place in this volunteer army, but mill-towns such as Carrick would have had a number

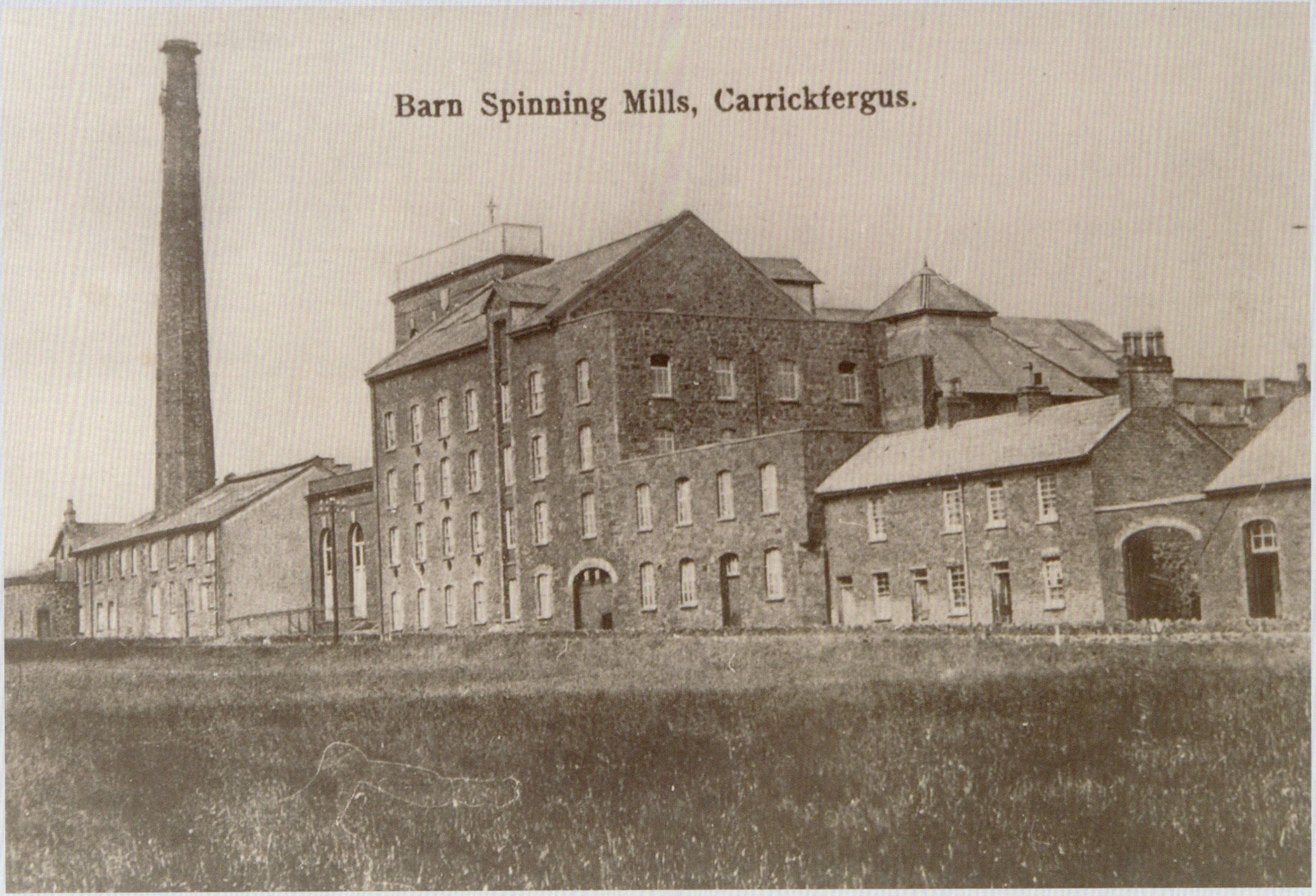

10

10. Barn Mills on Taylor's Avenue, from which several men went to the war.

of men whose health was too poor for active service, due to a legacy of bad nutrition and grim working-conditions.

Emotional scenes at the railway station occurred throughout the autumn. A reserve battalion of professional soldiers from the Royal Irish Fusiliers came to Sunnylands camp, upon the departure of the Yorkshiremen. Drafts of this new battalion were now being sent for training in England, prior to departure for France. As these Fusiliers caught the boat-train for Larne, the fife and drum band from their regiment played on the railway platform and crowds of local people sang such anthems as 'It's a Long Way to Tipperary' and 'Rule Britannia.'

Local men who had emigrated to far-off parts of the Empire, eventually responded to 'the call.' One volunteer was Thomas McMullan who had grown up in Carrickfergus and who travelled as a young man to Canada. He joined a Canadian Forestry battalion and sailed across the Atlantic for service at the front-line.

For several Carrickfergus citizens, the decision to fight the Germans was questionable – a sentiment found elsewhere in Ulster. The Ulster unionists had armed themselves in April 1914 with guns illegally procured in Germany. Louis MacNeice's sister would later recall that their housekeeper's father said 'he would as soon have the Kaiser as King George any day'. The old man claimed that the German monarch, Kaiser William II, was 'a good Protestant' and would be a defender of Ulster people against the dogmas of Catholicism and the resurgent forces of Irish nationalism.

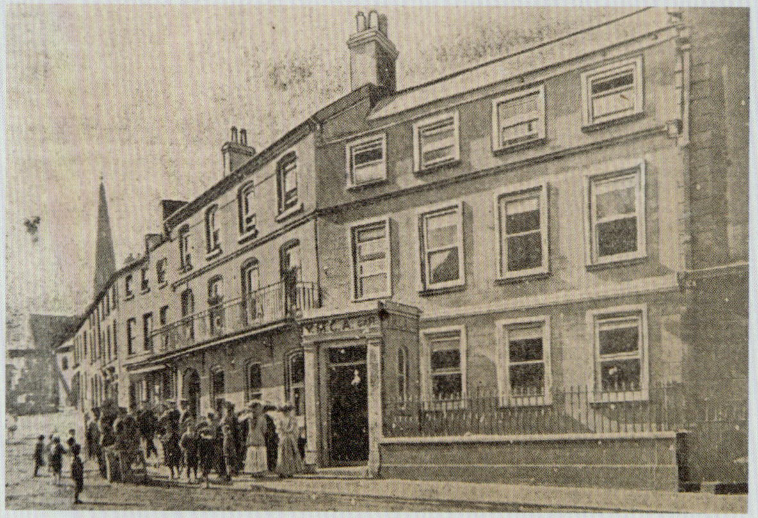

11

Despite the presence of such negative sentiments, local people were being encouraged by clergy, politicians and community leaders to 'get behind' the forces. The first of many war-time concerts was given in the Independent Hall in October to raise money for the 'Soldiers' and Sailors' Families Fund'. Another fund sent money to a military hospital in the French town of Pau, sponsored by the Ulster Volunteer Force. The gift was used to purchase a 'Carrickfergus bed'.

The Carrickfergus branch of the Young Mens' Christian Association was determined to offer assistance to servicemen stationed in and around the town. As well as facilities offered in their hall in the centre of the town, the YMCA provided refreshments, leisure activities and spiritual guidance to soldiers in a hut in Sunnylands. They extended their services to a tent at the

11. The YMCA offered help to soldiers at a number of local venues.
12. The little village of Eden had a strong military and maritime tradition.

bleak coastal locality where the Royal Garrison Artillery – including the locally recruited Antrim Artillery - had been manning their guns to defend the lough since the outbreak of war. As the local paper explained –

'A branch of the YMCA has recently been established at Kilroot Fort... a large marquee has been erected...[with] reading material on the tables. On Friday evening a number of friends from Carrickfergus visited the tent and provided an entertainment. It is intended to continue the concerts each week.'

Not everyone was happy with the presence of extra troops on the streets. One letter-writer to the local paper implored parents – *'I beg of you to look after your daughters at this time when temptations are in the way.'* However, reports of life for the local men who had gone as soldiers to Clandeboye, were very positive. Those who returned on leave seemed 'bronzed and healthy' due to outdoor life and physical training. And parcels were sent from Carrickfergus to Clandeboye, which contained soda bread, potato bread, socks, confectionary and cigarettes.

On 9th November, the town got a chance to see its men in military formation. The volunteers were now fully-fledged members of the 12th Royal Irish Rifles, and this battalion was undertaking a route march through County Antrim. The streets of Carrickfergus were lined with cheering crowds as the men marched into the town along the coast road from Belfast, passed the castle and the harbour and then headed onwards towards Whitehead. One section of the troops continued along the shoreline, through Eden and Kilroot, while another group of men travelled uphill along the 'old coach road' through Ballycarry, with its inspiring view of the Irish Sea and the distant Scottish coast.

As well as those volunteers who had joined the army, others followed local maritime traditions and joined the navy. One such was Edward James Robinson of Warwick's Row in Carrickfergus. Married in 1912, he left his wife in 1914 to do what he felt was his patriotic duty, joining the Royal Naval Reserve and subsequently entering the Merchant Navy, where he was a ship's carpenter. Many men also went to sea from Eden, Boneybefore and Whitehead. In a naval war which would feature submarines, mines and torpedoes, such service would come at a cost. Even before they faced the enemy, some local sailors paid the supreme price. In late November, a huge accidental explosion tore apart *HMS Bulwark*, whilst it was docked in Sheerness harbor. It claimed the life of Carrickfergus mariner, James Gardiner. He left behind a widow and two children.

Reports of other deaths soon appeared in the local paper. The demise of Samuel Johnston was particularly poignant. At one stage he had been an employee of the *Carrickfergus Advertiser*.

On the home front, the Defence of the Realm Act led to intrusive measures. Local pubs now had to endure restrictions on their opening hours, to prevent the effect of excess alcohol on workplace performance. The trains that snaked their way each night along the edge of the lough had strict orders to keep the blinds pulled down on carriage windows. This was to forestall any well-targeted aerial or naval bombardment by the enemy. The war was now striking home in significant ways.

Spirits were lifted by the arrival of the 12th Royal Irish Rifles, who were completing their tour of the county. 400 men were stationed for two nights in Whiteabbey, Larne and Ballyclare and 600 in Carrickfergus. Existing

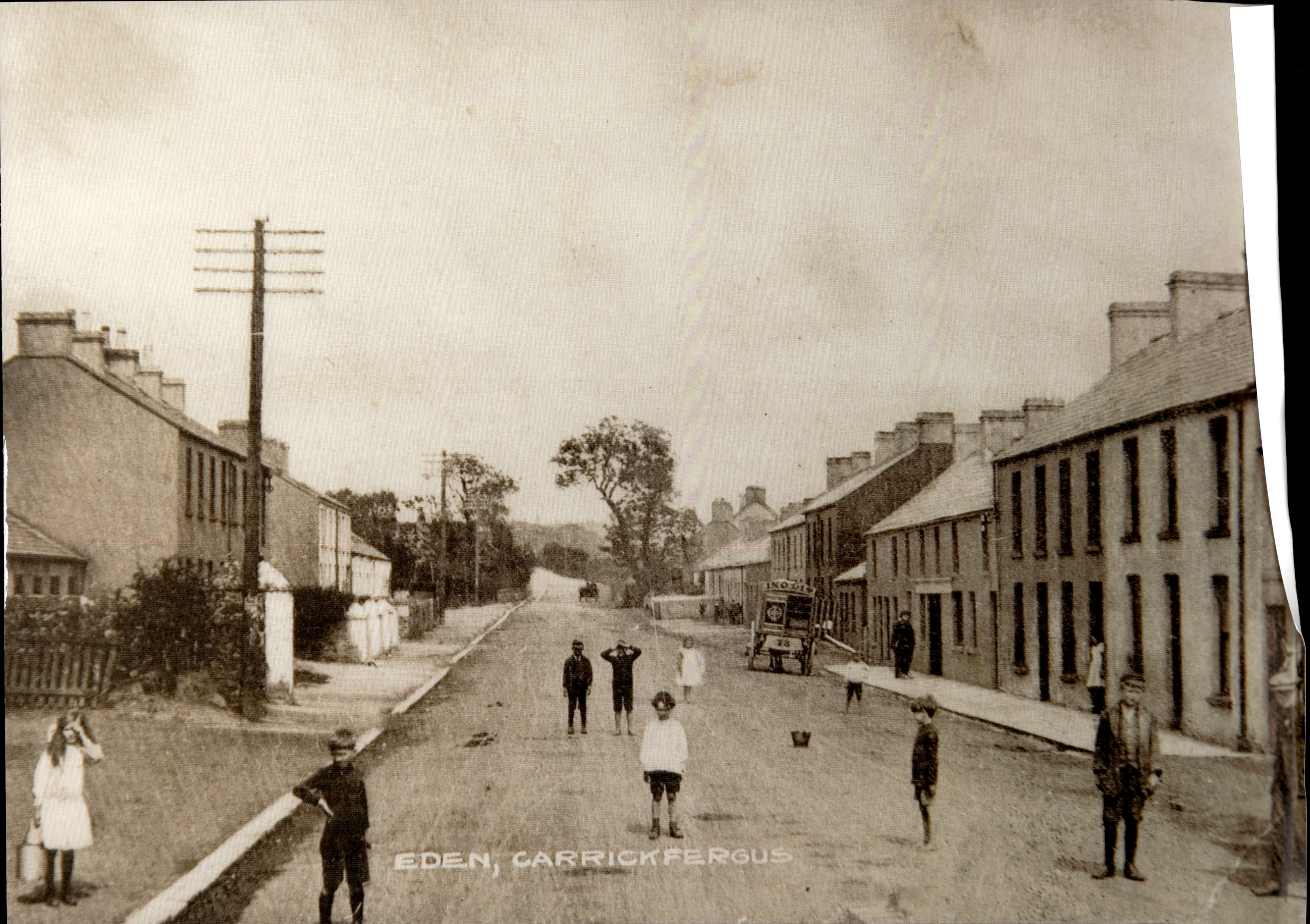

EDEN, CARRICKFERGUS

military accommodation was full to overflowing at Sunnylands and at the old 18th century courthouse where the artillerymen had their base. As a result, the men were billeted in numerous houses around the town over the weekend, with some homes taking up to twelve guests! The arrival of these men caused excitement. They marched from Larne via the 'Snowy Glen', with its vista across the lough to the northern shores of County Down. Then they descended towards Carrickfergus across the 'Great Commons' and entered along the North Road into the town.

That weekend, 'smoking concerts' and other entertainments were held for the troops. On Sunday morning, all the church services were well attended. Then on a wet, cool Monday morning, the troops left Carrickfergus and marched along the seafront through Greenisland, then on towards Belfast, accompanied for part of the way by the band of the Royal Irish Fusiliers.

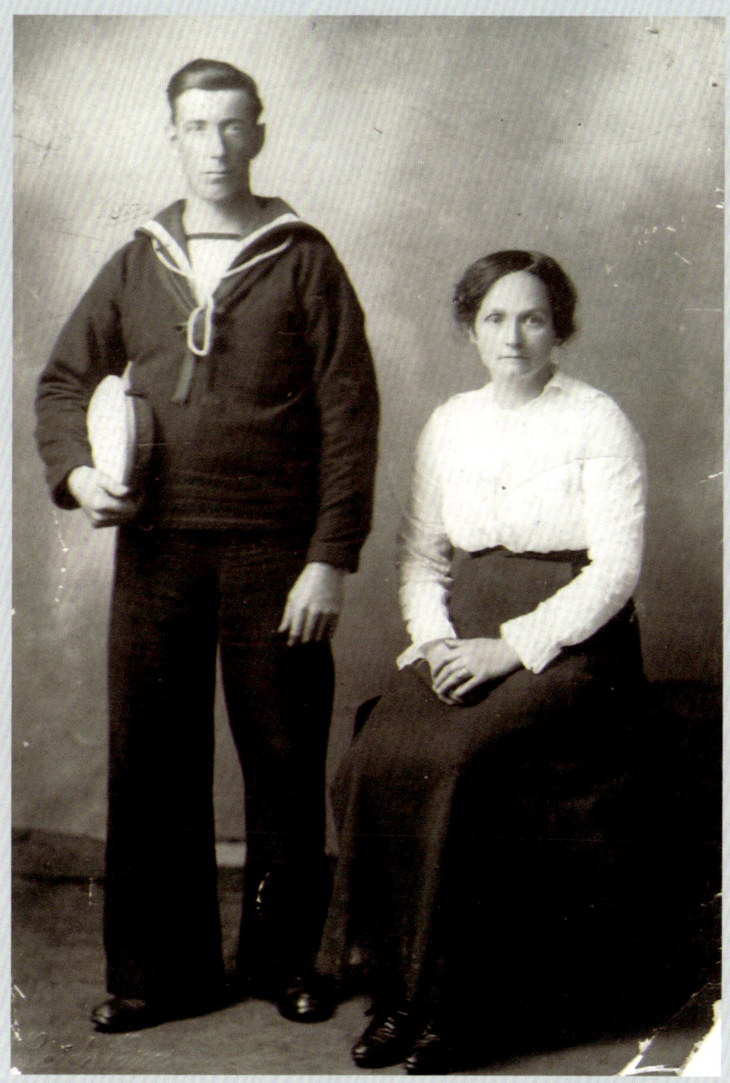
13

13. Edward James Robinson with his wife. He volunteered for wartime service with the navy.

1915

By 1915, the 4th battalion of Royal Irish Fusiliers was proving popular in wartime Carrickfergus. This unit contained men from Cavan and Monaghan, largely Catholic by background and in all probability nationalist in their sympathies. It was a reserve battalion, devoted to preparing new recruits for the front and performing a range of domestic duties. There were few tensions in their relationship with the Protestant majority in the town. The spiritual and physical needs of the Fusiliers were catered for by the Catholic community at St Nicholas Catholic Church. At Christmas a supper had been provided in the church school.

The Fusiliers were known as 'the bhoys' and they called at Bell's shop where copies of local newspapers were obtained, having been sent to County Antrim by train. Bell's was always busy. At no stage was it more vibrant than in the run-up to St Patrick's Day in 1915, when orders were placed for shamrock to be shipped to soldiers serving abroad. The shop displayed items of interest in its window. These included some butter knives, made out of bullets - a wartime souvenir, sent back by a local soldier, William Skelton. There was also the ghoulish exhibit of a pair of scissors found in the hand of a dead German nurse whose head had apparently been blown off by a shell!

Also available for local viewing was the album of Sister McCloskey, who returned on leave from nursing duties on board a hospital ship, the *Karafara*. The *Advertiser* revealed that this album contained 'signatures of many of her patients.' After the war, Louis MacNeice's father compiled a list of 17 women – including Sister McCloskey – who 'left home to serve'.

A plaque in Whitehead Presbyterian Church records the war service of three women in that congregation.

Romance blossomed between local girls and soldiers. Bernard Murtagh from Killeshandra, County Cavan, became very friendly with a local dressmaker. In February, he received news that he was in the next draft for the front.

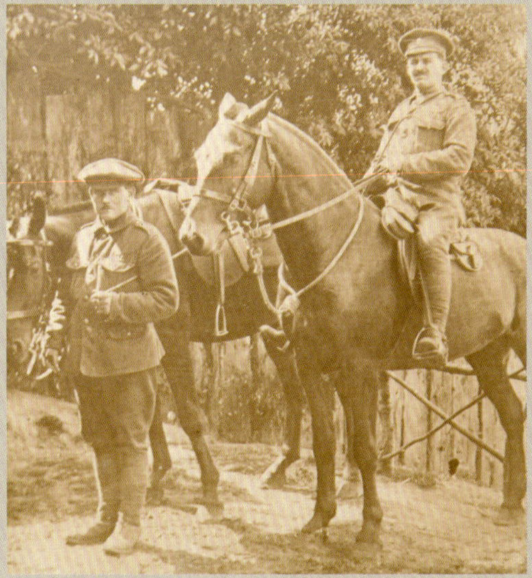

14

14. The soldier on horseback is a Royal Irish Fusilier, Bernard Murtagh from County Cavan.
He looked after his officer's horse, among other duties.
15. The 'big lamp' and Bell's shop – important gathering places in wartime Carrickfergus.

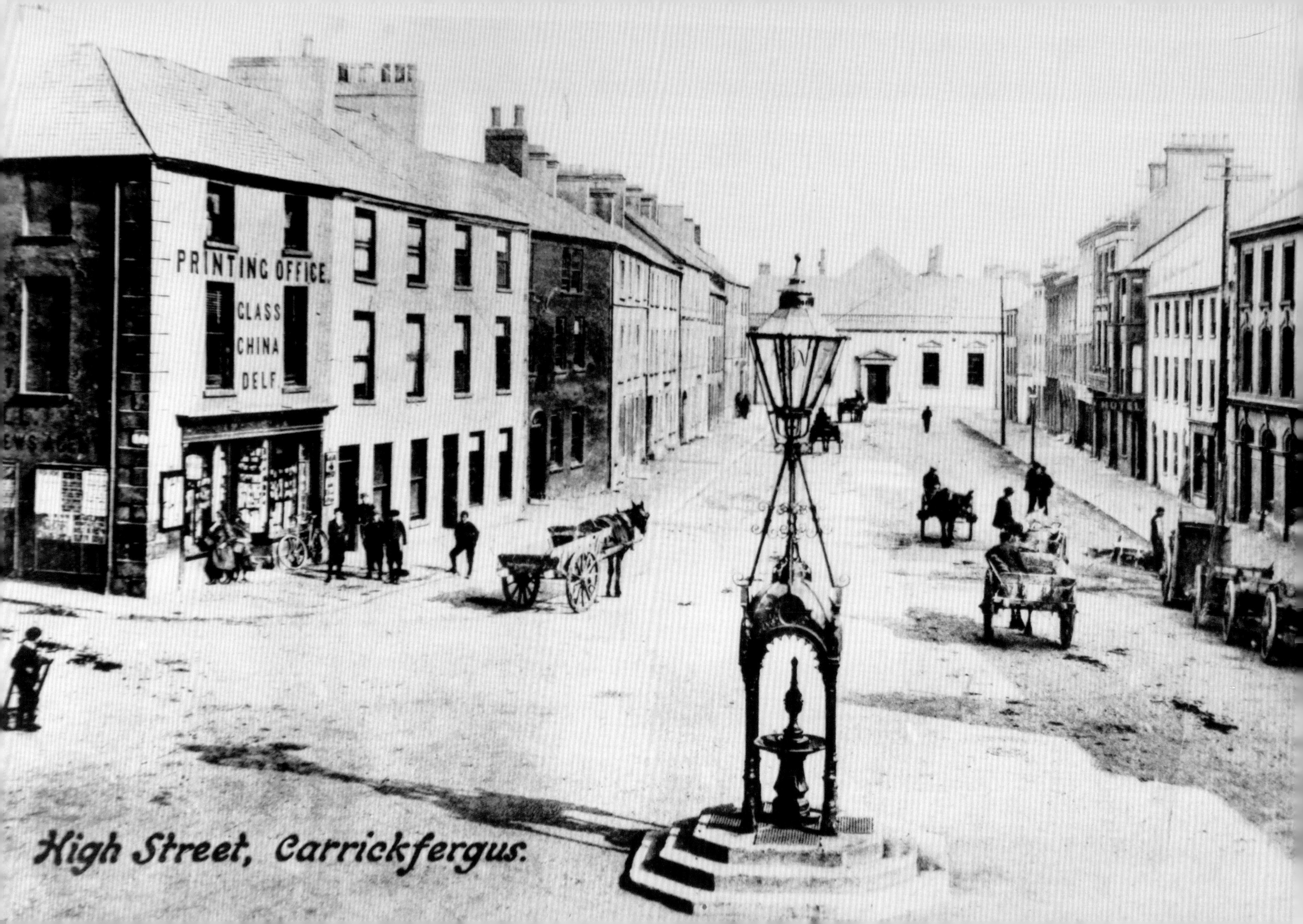

High Street, Carrickfergus.

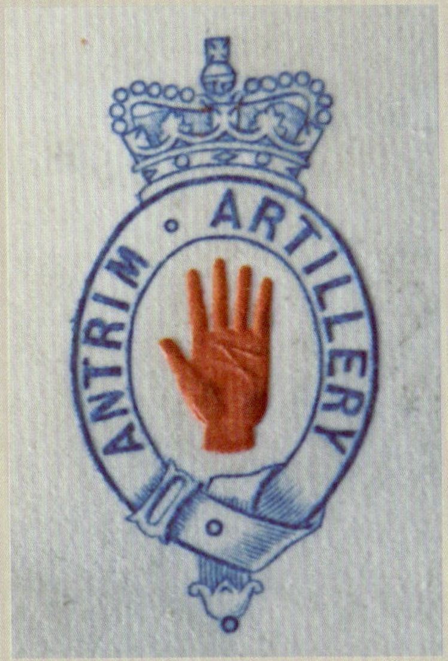

16

The young couple went to Father Henry, the parish priest, asking to be married. On Sunday February 14th - Valentine's Day – the ceremony took place. On the following day, Bernard went to the station after bidding farewell to his bride. He felt a hand on his shoulder, and heard the familiar voice of an officer telling him - 'You're off the draft!'.

Father Henry had 'had a word' with the authorities and the newly married Cavan man was allowed a 'honeymoon' before he was sent abroad in March.

Father Henry felt that he operated in a part of Ulster which possessed good 'community relations', despite the recent tensions of the Home Rule crisis. At the dedication of the new Catholic church in Whitehead, in 1909, he had spoken of 'those protestant gentlemen... who were present' at the ceremony and others who 'sent generous subscriptions' for the erection of the building.

But recruitment in Ireland during 1915 was slackening. News of the casualties at the front-line made an impact on earlier enthusiasm. The conflict was bogged down in attritional trench warfare and horrible new weapons were making an appearance, such as poison gas. So a detachment of the 4th Royal Irish Fusiliers returned from Cavan and Monaghan where they had been on a recruitment tour, reporting little success. Posters were also placed in windows of premises throughout Carrickfergus and Whitehead and articles appeared in the local newspaper, enticing more local men to 'join up'. A recruiting drive was planned for the annual hiring fair, when a considerable number of young men came to the town from the surrounding country districts, looking for work. Twenty lads volunteered on the day of the fair in 1915. However, the opportunities for hired farm workers had never been better, as agricultural output expanded to meet the needs of a country at war. And so recruitment among the lads of rural County Antrim was in reality rather meagre. However some statistics, dealt with later in this account, reveal that the overall recruitment rates along the northern shores of Belfast Lough were actually relatively high.

Not all casualties occurred overseas, as the community found out on 24th April On that night, William Ruddy and his friend, James O'Hara, who were stationed at Kilroot, had been granted a 'pass' and walked into Whitehead for

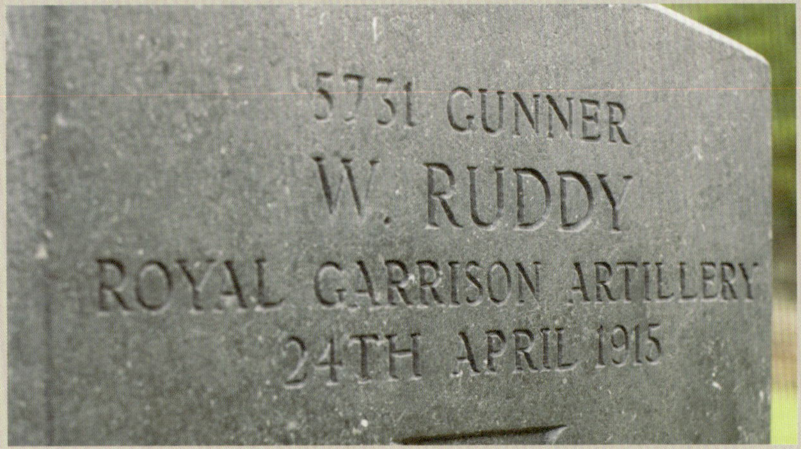

17

16. The badge of the Antrim Artillery.
17. Private Ruddy's gravestone, in the Victoria Road cemetery.

a few drinks. After consuming their liquor, probably in the Railway Bar, close to the station, the men walked back to Kilroot along the railway line. As they were late, O'Hara speeded up, leaving Ruddy to stumble along in his wake. While O'Hara arrived in time, Ruddy did not. The driver of a locomotive, which was making its way along the Larne line from Carrickfergus, felt his train collide with an unidentified object. He brought the vehicle to a halt.

Ruddy's mutilated body was scattered over the tracks.

On the following Tuesday, his remains were carried on a gun carriage through the ironwork gateway of the Victoria cemetery, accompanied by a military guard and firing party. Draped on the coffin was a Union Jack, on which were placed a helmet and sword of the Royal Garrison Artillery. A band played the 'Dead March from Saul' and a bugler played the Last Post.

The thoughts of the public were soon focused on other issues. The Royal Irish Fusiliers were leaving Sunnylands in May, replaced by a reserve unit of the Royal Irish Rifles. At St Nicholas Catholic Church, a farewell for the men was organized by Father Henry, at the close of which the National Anthem was sung. On the following day, the Royal Irish Fusiliers marched along the coast road to a barracks in Belfast, accompanied for part of the way by friends from the town. The local paper lamented their departure and relished the fact that during their stay, 'the bhoys' had been given 'Cead mile failte' (Irish for '100,000 welcomes')

On 8th May there was an opportunity to travel by train to Belfast and watch the 36th Division perform a grand march through the city - an occasion tinged with sadness because, before long, the Ulstermen would move to England for further training. Local men in the 12th Royal Irish Rifles looked more than ever like real soldiers, marching smartly past the City Hall behind their regimental band, which played military airs, including the battalion's 'signature tune', King Wiliam's March.

Most troops were granted home leave before the division headed for Sussex. As goodbyes were said at the station there was little sign of the jollity which had characterised the initial departures for Clandeboye. Instead, groups of friends and family engaged in tearful farewells on the platform.

Wartime life continued as before. The attempt to enlist new soldiers did not slacken. Organizers of a 'recruitment parade' on the Whitehead Esplanade tried to gather in some of the holiday-makers in the seaside town. However,

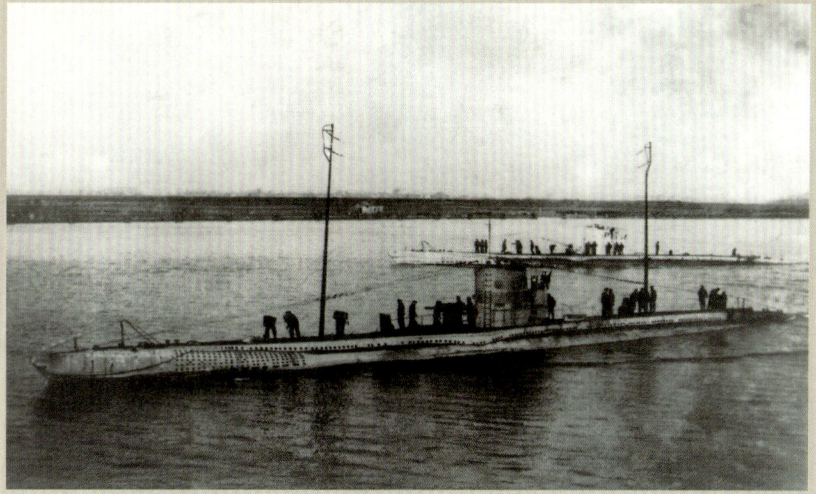
18

18. U-boats often appeared in County Antrim's offshore waters.

for many men, army life was not appealing, as the *Carrickfergus Advertiser* noted in early July –

'A large number of husky male individuals are standing around the 'big lamp' in Victoria Square every night with no intention of serving their country, to calmly discuss the greatest European War from an abstract point of view, as if it did not matter one iota whether the Germans came to Carrick or not.'

The thought that Germans might 'come to Carrick' was not entirely far-fetched. The British feared raids on coastal locations. These included Kilroot Fort and the ordnance stores in Carrickfergus. Gunships had bombarded English towns such as Scarborough. Submarine assaults on shipping had become very frequent – including the sinking of the *Lusitania*, off the Irish coast, in April. Fishermen, operating by lamplight near Greenisland, were apprehended in June, on the suspicion that they were spies, signaling to a U-boat. And some local people expressed concern about the visibility to enemy shipping of car headlights on the coast road.

For some Carrickfergus residents, war was an opportunity to make money. In June, James McGookin of Castle Street was arrested for 'giving or selling drink to soldiers on duty.' Band members of the 4th Royal Irish Rifles had formed a habit of retiring to McGookin's house, once they had led the troops to church parade on Sundays. Police entered this house and reported finding 'six soldiers, wearing cross-belts...drinking porter out of bottles or glasses.'

However, most people in the locality were simply making do with the straitened circumstances brought by war. Sugar, butter and meat would all be rationed during the conflict And as coal became expensive, turf became a popular fuel – the price of the cheapest coal available in Carrick rose from 19 shillings per ton to 36 shillings per ton in the course of the war.

For some citizens, the tragedy of war was becoming all too real. In July sad news arrived for Mrs Gillespie of Whitehead. She had received information about her son, Norman. Like many men from the vicinity, he had emigrated to Canada to find work, adventure and opportunity. When war came, he enlisted with a Canadian regiment. Drafted to Flanders in Belgium, he was gassed at Ypres. Captured by the enemy, he perished from respiratory illness on 25th April 1915. The news was passed on to the Gillespie family by the Red Cross in Geneva.

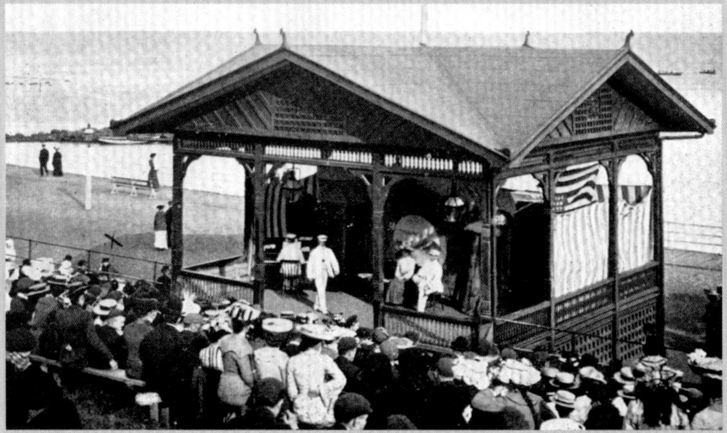

19

One Carrickfergus family averted tragedy in 1915. Their son was sent home. The authorities had found out that he was under-age. The boy returned from the Dardanelles in the Eastern Mediterranean, where Irish troops were

19. A pierrot show on the Whitehead Esplanade.
20. The Poppinjays - a popular performing troupe in wartime Whitehead.

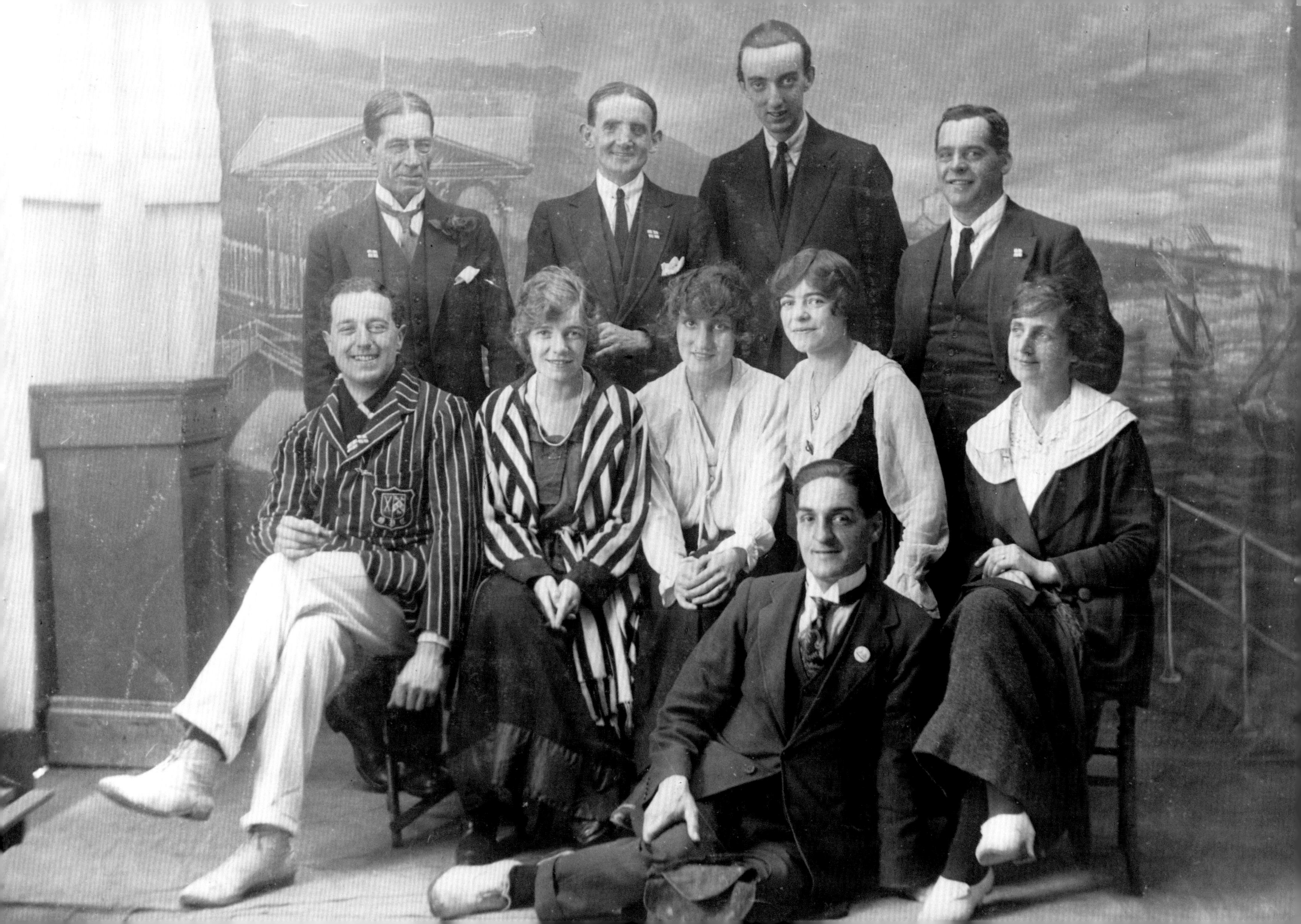

involved in an attempt to knock Germany's ally, Turkey, out of the war. The lad was 16 when he was sent back to Ireland and he could have been as young as 14 when he was admitted to the army.

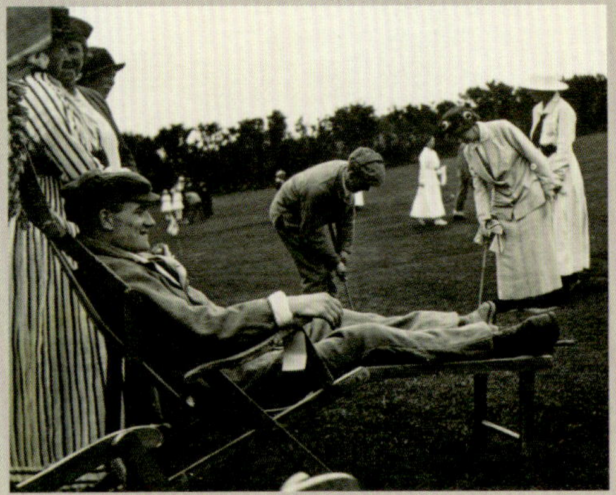
21

Throughout the summer, Whitehead provided a popular holiday destination for many Ulster people, despite the ongoing European conflict. The highlight of the season was the arrival of a theatre company called The Poppinjays, many of whose performers were based in London's Savoy Theatre. Their show, entitled *Stardust*, was staged in the Esplanade Pavilion – a marquee erected at the sea-front. The show was booked out each night.

Some of the men in the audience were no doubt soldiers who had been to the front and suffered injury. The process of recuperation was often a slow one and Whitehead provided the Merview convalescent home for such veterans, situated on the hill-slopes overlooking the bay. Sunnylands camp also had residential facilities for recuperating soldiers. A common feature of their rehabilitation was a day-trip or an entertainment.

The local paper recorded in early August that –

'over fifty wounded soldiers from the Belfast hospitals spent a pleasant afternoon on Friday as the guests of the Whitehead Golf Club – at least one "stalwart lad" showed that he was just as much at home with a putter in his hands as a rifle...'

21. A putting competition for injured soldiers at Bentra.

The putting event was followed by 'quoite-throwing competitions' and the prizes mainly consisted of cigarettes.

By the mid-August, news arrived from Seaford in Sussex, where the Ulster Division was based. The *Carrickfergus Advertiser* published a poem, written by Thomas Cooke, Robert Smyth, William Rooney, Charles Thomas and Francis Robinson, all serving in No 6 platoon of B company in the 12th Rifles.

'Just a year ago today
Earl Kitchener made the call,
And the good young blood of Carrick town
Responded one and all.

They've got a few good rifles,
And some shining bayonets too,
To mow the traitorous Germans down,
That's what they hope to do.

In the pretty town of Seaford,
They are waiting on the word
To advance upon the murderous Hun,
Like true-born Irish sons.

How will the baby-killers feel
When they get some Irish steel
For the Carrick boys will use their guns
Nor spare no mercy for the Huns.

We have got a noble leader,
Who is well-known in our town,
Lieutenant Lemon is his name –
A man of high renown.

Then comes our gallant colonel,
Whom we work for with all skill.
To lead us o'er the plains of France,
No doubt he surely will.

Now as our time is drawing near,
And we are soon to roam,
We'll bid adieu to all our friends
In the dear old Irish home.'

When autumn approached, the 36th Division was thrust from training camps in the south of England into the French battlefields of the Western Front. There was plenty of evidence in barracks towns such as Carrickfergus, of the dangers they now faced. Numerous disabled soldiers, who had been injured at the front in the early months of the war, were to be seen making their way from Sunnylands through the streets. Some were in wheelchairs, some were hobbling about on crutches and others were suffering from the loss of an eye. Some had lost at least one limb.

Many of these men came from all across the British Isles. However there was a growing list of local casualties. In August, the Kerr family of West Street received news that their boy David had been injured in the Dardanelles. A member of the rowing club and former captain of Carrickfergus rugby team, he had moved to Dublin to work for the Irish Land Commission, where he joined the keen sportsmen in the Royal Dublin Fusiliers known as the Dublin Pals. Many had been slaughtered in the landings at Suvla Bay on the Gallipoli peninsula.

The Butler family of Fairymount suffered even more badly in the conflict. Mrs Butler lost two sons and a stepson, all of whom had been pre-war 'regular' soldiers. Martin had been killed at Hooge, John was fatally wounded at Mons and James had lost his life at the Dardanelles. By September 1915, Carrickfergus and its environs had lost 13 men killed, 20 men wounded and one man taken prisoner of war.

However, life had to go on. The factory hooter sounded every day at the Barn Mills, horses carried rock-salt from local mines to ships moored at the quays and bathing-parties of soldiers took part in 'aquatic events' in the harbour, including 'plunging competitions' and '100 yard swimming races'.

One amusing story surfaced in October. The German Kaiser had presented King Edward VII with a statue of William III (William of Orange) in 1907. There was uncertainty in governmental circles about where to place this gift. A movement had started in Carrickfergus to have it placed above the North Gate in the town, in remembrance of William's 17th century arrival at the harbour, on his way to fight the famous Battle of the Boyne. It was noted with relief and amusement that nothing had come of the plan and that the statue now stood at Kensington Palace.

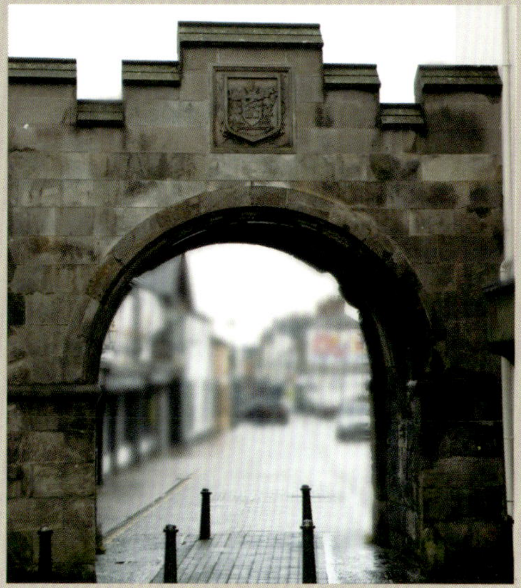
22

Carrickfergus had escaped the misfortune of having its name coupled with that of the Kaiser.

By November the Ulster Division was adapting to the trenches, with their rats and lice and ongoing threat of shellfire or a sniper's deadly bullets. The men were becoming familiar with poor food and the discomfort of sentry duty on cold nights, the claustrophobic dug-outs where they slept when 'in the line' and the bare barns where they lay when 'off duty'. Men were acquainted with the challenge of night-time

22. To the amusement of local people, they learnt that in the pre-war years, the North Gate had narrowly escaped being the location for a statue of William III, presented to the British people by the Kaiser.

raids on enemy lines and the use of their Lee-Enfield rifle and their grenades, known as Mills Bombs.

Letters from the front arrived – censored for information that could affect morale or reveal secrets. Men who could not compose letters sent 'field postcards', which gave reassurance to loved ones that they were alive and well.

In early November, news broke of the first 36th Divisional death in the trenches. The man's family resided in Monkstown and originally came from Carrickfergus. Samuel Hill, who was killed on 22nd October, had played football for Barn Swifts. A memorial service was held in Joymount Presbyterian church, with which his family had been connected. The Reverend Minford preached on the verse – 'Greater love hath no man than this, that a man should lay down his life for his friends'. He commented on the patriotic duty shown by the Hills – who also had a boy in the navy. Samuel Hill was buried at Doullens cemetery in France, under a wooden Celtic cross, on which was written the inscription –

'First man of the Division to give his life for his King and country and for the honour of Ulster.'

By Christmas, photos of Hill's grave appeared in the window of Bells' shop.

Not all news from France was sad. One group of lads in the 36th Division wrote home, describing concerts they had improvised behind the lines. The letter was headed with the address – 'The Drafty Villa, Frostbite Avenue, France' and the program included 'a clog dance by R.Rooney (the bully-beef wrestler)...an imitation of Charlie Chaplin by S.Kyle (the soda farl swallower) and a song by D.McQuitty (the biscuit juggler) entitled 'Why I left my home'.'

Another letter to the local paper requested the 'good people' of Carrickfergus to send a melodeon to the 'Carrick men' in the army, so that they could 'pass the dreary nights' with music. One other letter enclosed a photograph of a woman which had been found in trenches where 'Carrick men' had been on duty. The editor of the *Advertiser* enjoyed drawing attention to the fact that the girl in question was 'Miss Jean McFerran of Irish Quarter West...a young lady whose smiling face is well known to callers at the Post office.'

Another poem appeared locally in the winter of 1915. Yet again the author was from 'No.6 platoon' and the location was 'somewhere in France.'

We came from dear old Carrick,
A town of high renown.
Better boys could not be found
If you travelled the whole world round.

Our captain's name is Murray
Of whom we're very fond.
With Captain Johns to help him,
We can lick the Kaiser's crowd.

Then comes Lieutenant Lemon,
A man who you all know,
Will lead the famous number 6
No matter where they go.

Come all you Ulster slackers,
And join our ranks – be men-
Do as your chums before you did,
For your chance won't come again.

And when the war is over,
And we are homeward bound
We are sure of a hearty welcome
In dear old Carrick town.

As the second Christmas of wartime approached, local families constantly awaited news from the front. Often the information that arrived was of a fearfully partial kind. The Rice family of Warwick's Row knew their boy Archie had gone missing on 7th August with the 10th (Irish) Division at the Dardanelles. No word had been received to indicate whether he was dead or alive.

There was sad news for the congregation of St Nicholas Catholic church, as the festive season approached. Father Henry had died, whilst in his early 50's, on 14th December. Detachments of the Royal Garrison Artillery and Royal Irish Rifles, to whom the priest had been chaplain, drew up on either side of the avenue leading to the church. They came to attention as his remains were borne to the tiny tree-lined graveyard beside the chapel.

For poor inhabitants of the town, Christmas was not anticipated with any relish. There was a problem all through the war-years with small boys who ran through Carrickfergus, thieving nuggets of coal from the carts that made their way into town from the harbour. Throughout the winter months, children from the most disadvantaged parts of the town scavenged food from Sunnylands. They made their way through gaps in the perimeter fence. On one occasion, guards tried to apprehend them. Although the men retrieved 'three loaves of bread, a 6lb tin of bully beef and a just-opened pot of jam', the children 'threw stones and called filthy names at the men' as they ran away.

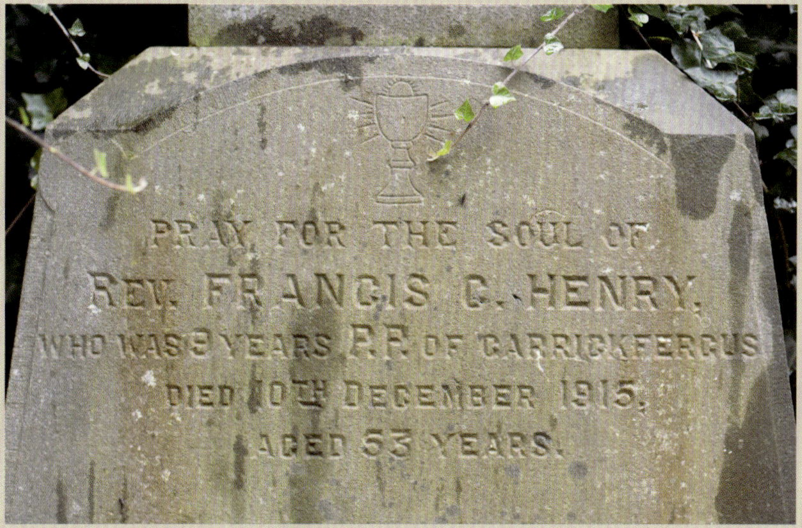

23

23. Father Henry's grave in the grounds of St. Nicholas Catholic Church.
He was a chaplain to many of the troops until his death, late in 1915.

1916

Interaction between Carrickfergus people and men at the front continued in 1916. Gifts made their way to the trenches and Barn football club sent footballs to their friends in 'B' Company of the 12th Rifles. Soldiers on leave brought news of their comrades. Captain Adamson, returning to Whitehead, spoke of excellent morale in the 36th Division, saying there was 'neither wavering or doubt' and that the men were 'known among the Huns as Carson's Boys'.

Ulster Division troops were not the only ones to keep in touch with Carrickfergus. Letters arrived from some of the Royal Irish Fusiliers who had been stationed at Sunnylands, including a correspondent who was now with the 10th (Irish)Division in Serbia and vowed - 'If I ever get to Ireland, I will make it my business to visit Carrickfergus...' Finding out that men in this battalion had lost their shaving kits, the editor of the *Advertiser* asked readers to 'help out' and send shaving equipment to their 'old friends.'

Father McKay, the new priest at Mount St Nicholas, corresponded with men in the forces. He struck up a friendship with local man, Captain W.H.Davey, a barrister and journalist who had won the OBE for his work, had been a member of Queens University Officer Training Corps, and who now served with the Tyneside Irish Brigade of the Northumberland Fusiliers. As a result, £5 was sent from his parishioners to Davey's platoon. Expressing his thanks, Davey wrote to say that the Tyneside Irish were 'worthy sons of the old sod'. Father McKay replied that 'If this is anybody's war it is Ireland's, for it is the war of freedom...'

Not everyone in Ireland agreed.

At Easter, many local people were shocked to learn that an armed rebellion against British rule had broken out in Dublin, led by Patrick Pearse and James Connolly, for whom the war was seen as a blood-sacrifice of young Irishmen on behalf of an alien empire. Although the insurgents were defeated, the centre of the Irish capital lay in ruins. Before long, rebel leaders had been tried and executed. The shock waves reverberated as far as County Antrim. Many public figures in the town vigorously condemned the rising, including the rector of St. Nicholas Church of Ireland, for whom it was treachery in time of war.

For the Catholic population of the area – and for some Protestants - reaction to the Easter Rising and its suppression was probably more complex. Anyone who had nationalist inclinations felt some sympathy with the ideals of the Easter Rising, if not the methods. A strong sense of resurgent 'Irishness' did exist here and there in the locality, as indicated by the presence of a Gaelic League in Carrickfergus since 1901. The League was dedicated to promoting such key features of indigenous Celtic culture as the Irish language. Despite close ties between St. Nicholas Catholic Church and the military life of the town, the fact that the Easter Rising had been inspired by intense Irish patriotism and was so vigorously suppressed by the British government, would have been a source of concern to those local Catholics who possessed strong nationalist sympathies. The fact that some members of the local

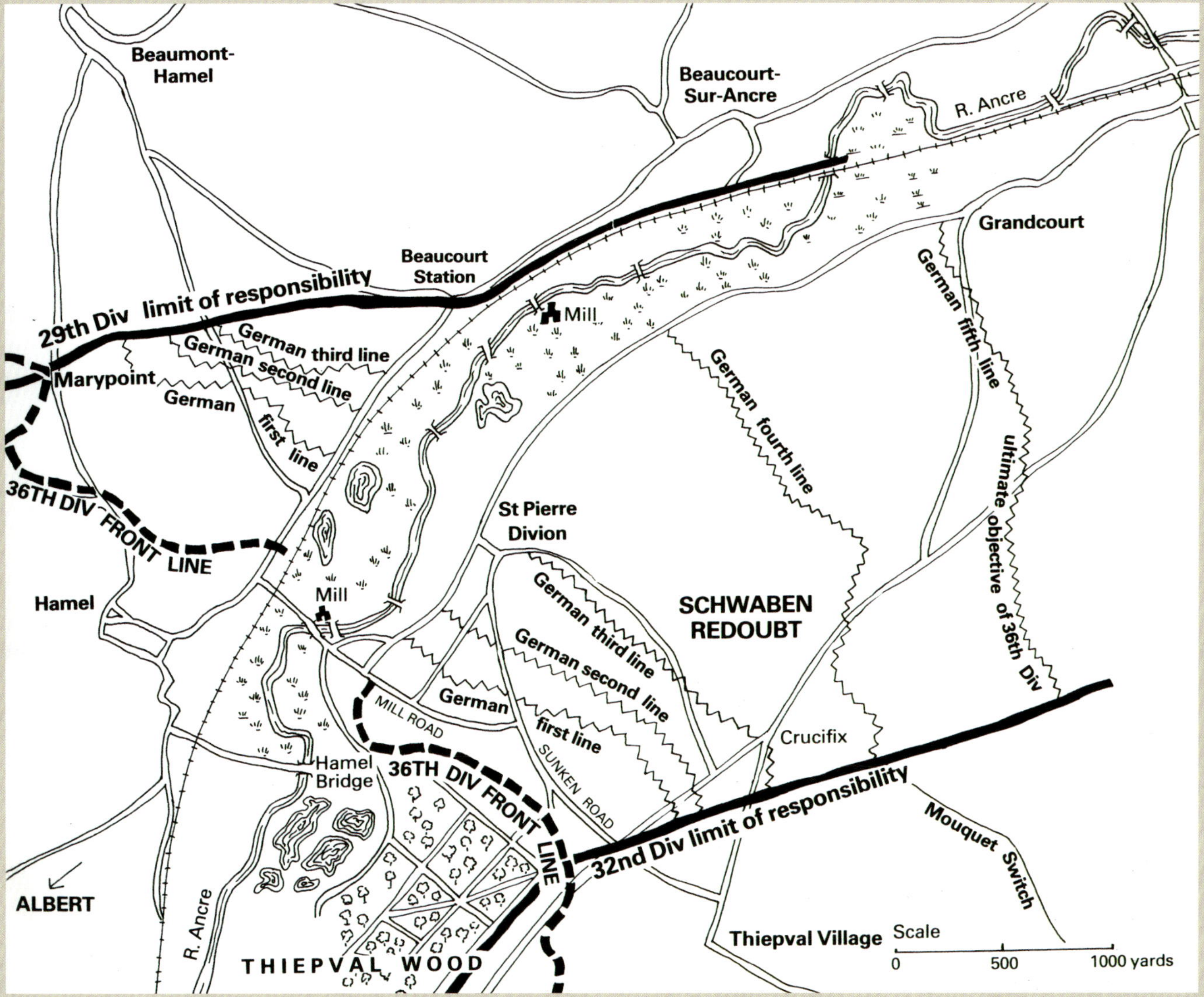

24

24. The objectives of the 36th Ulster Division on 1st July 1916. Many local men were fighting in the sector seen to the north of the River Ancre on this map.

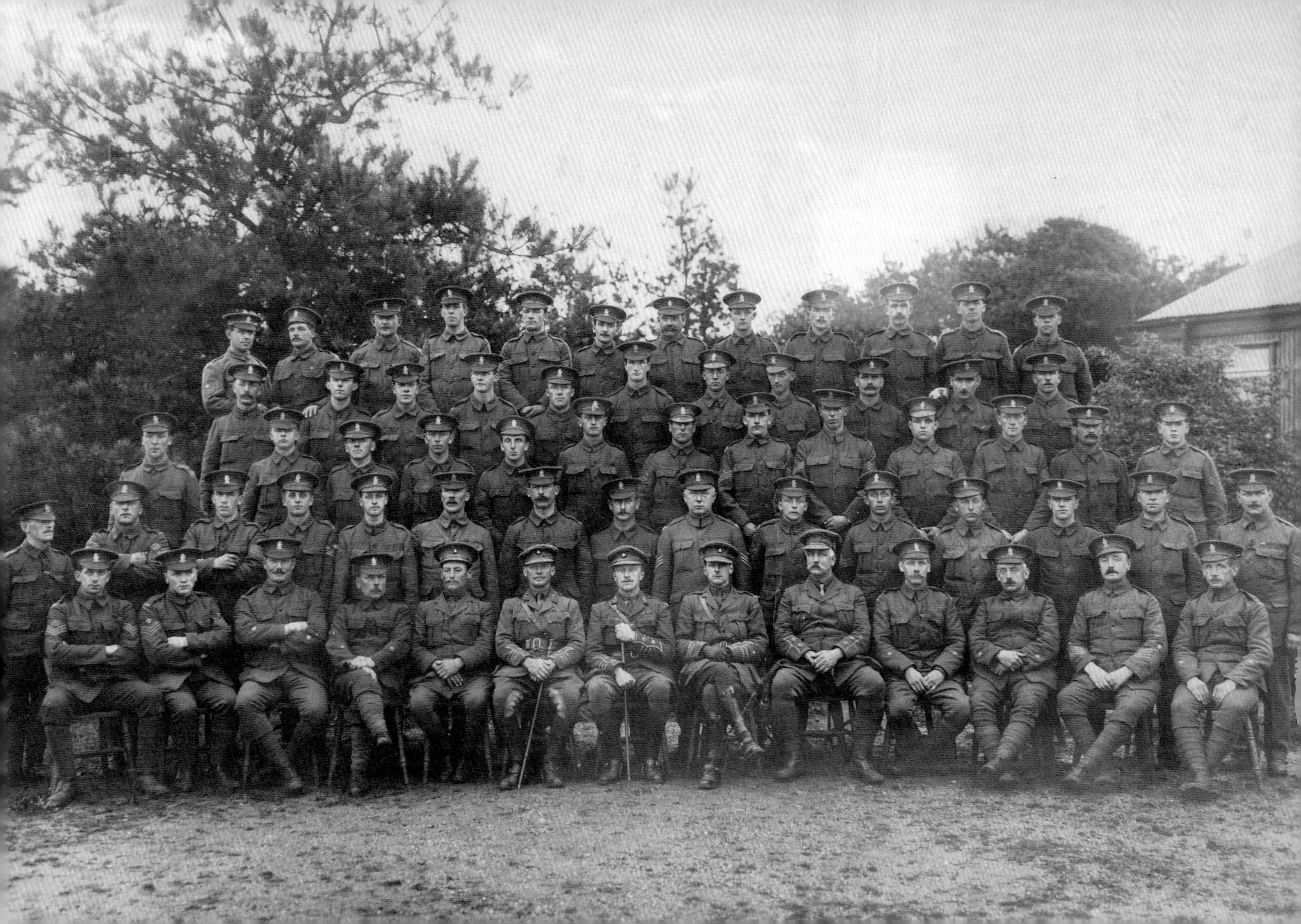

garrison regiment, the 4th Royal Irish Rifles, had been involved in quelling the insurrection, would have added to the difficulties.

However, throughout the spring and early summer of 1916, the Easter Rising made little impact on everyday life in this part of Ulster. In Whitehead, residents started to prepare for the holiday season. South-east County Antrim - undisturbed by civil strife - was also oblivious to the huge offensive being contemplated on the Western Front, centred on the Somme region. It was a battle in which local men were ordered to play a part.

The Somme offensive was designed to break the stalemate. An artillery bombardment would pulverise enemy positions and men of Lord Kitchener's 'New Army' would march across and occupy the German lines. After that it would be a matter of heading into open countryside and marching towards the German capital, Berlin. The 36th Division had been given the role of attacking Germans on either side of the River Ancre. To the north of the river, the 9th Royal Irish Fusiliers and 12th Royal Irish Rifles were asked to cross a ravine and advance up a slope towards German trenches, beyond which lay a railway station. The sixth and eighth platoons of B company – containing many Carrick men - would operate close to the river and nearby railway line. On 24th June, bombardment began. Carrickfergus and Whitehead men, like every other soldier in the Somme sector, prepared themselves for battle amidst the din of shellfire. They would enter the battlefield, carrying a load of military kit as well as a rifle, a bayonet and hand grenades.

A soldier with the 12th Royal Irish Rifles was present at a burial service on 29th June, when a dying enemy soldier was brought in from no man's land to where the battalion was stationed, behind the lines. Later he would recall the experience and the melancholy questions that he was asking himself about the war – questions that never surfaced in the usual cheery letters home.

'The rain stopped that day and we were asked to dig a grave for him in a corner of a field where we buried our own dead. There was two men of the 12th rifles being buried that same day. It still sticks in my mind that a Protestant pastor said the same burial service over the three men. I wondered what in hell we were doing fighting one another. After all we were all men, only the uniform was different. That night there was a glorious sunset. The guns were silent for a while and I heard someone in the reserve trenches start to sing 'Abide with me'. Then slowly all down the line the men took up the hymn. For about fifteen minutes we sang hymns.'

On 1st July, at 7.30 am, bombardment ceased and the infantry assault began. North of the Ancre the 9th Fusiliers and 12th Rifles scrambled out of front line trenches and headed for their objectives. They did not know that enemy dug-outs were deep and strong and that the Germans had been safe within them throughout the bombardment. What is more, the enemy may well have been aware of the time when the infantry attack would start, due to expert surveillance. The Germans rose from their shelters, manned machine guns and prepared their bayonets and grenades for close quarter combat.

Both the Fusiliers and the Rifles sustained serious casualties from the moment they left their lines. Those who struggled across the ravine and reached the barbed wire found it an intimidating barrier, containing barbs the length of a man's thumb. Men made for gaps in the wire, to find that the Germans had trained their guns on those particular spots.

25. Two platoons from B company in the 12th Royal Irish Rifles, which suffered so heavily on 1st July. Many local men were in this company.

Number 6 platoon was ordered to penetrate the Railway Sap, a trench extending into no man's land, at right angles to enemy lines, close to the railway. Even before the ravine had been reached, many men dropped to the ground, hit by bullets issuing from machine-guns which fired 400 rounds a minute. Lieutenant Archibald Lemon led No 6 platoon from the ravine into the sap but swiftly became a casualty. A handful of the platoon managed to push on and enter the first line of German trenches. They were trapped and outnumbered. Eventually only two survivors were left. They turned and headed across no man's land towards safety.

By 2pm, all the men who survived the attack on the German lines north of the Ancre were back in their own trenches and were relieved by English troops at 6.30pm. 600 men out of 1,000 troops who were registered with the 12th Royal Irish Rifles had been selected to mount the attack on the Germans on 1st July. Approximately 450 were casualties. 150 had been killed and 300 injured.

There had been a 75% attrition rate.

South of the river, the rest of the division also experienced heavy losses and over 2,000 Ulster soldiers died in a single day. Elsewhere on the Somme, thousands of volunteers in Lord Kitchener's New Army had perished.

The corpses of several Carrickfergus men were never found. Some had been blown to pieces by shellfire. Other corpses sank into the ground near the river or deteriorated on the bare slopes of no man's land. Among those 'missing believed killed' were Edward Carlisle, aged 29 from Minorca Place, Thomas Clarke, aged 26, of Victoria Terrace, and George Owens, aged 21, of Albert Road. Owens had been an apprentice fitter in pre-war life and his parents and nine siblings were left to grieve over his loss.

Also missing were Thomas Partridge, Robert Patterson, John McIlwaine, James McCarthy, Francis Kirk and Hugh Kerr. Missing too was the body of 41 year-old Lieutenant Archibald Lemon, who before the war had lived in Strandtown in East Belfast. As a former manager at the Barn Mills, he led several of his employees within No 6 platoon in the attempt to penetrate the Railway Sap, which had been such a hopeless venture.

At home, news from the Somme penetrated the newspapers. By the second half of July it was clear that there had been heroism and heavy losses in the Ulster Division. Telegram-boys were awaited with trepidation, carrying the envelopes which bore news that yet another home had been visited by tragedy. Casualty lists appeared in the local newspapers and were posted in the window of Bells' shop and other newsagents, so that those who could not afford a paper might read the details. Illiterate citizens asked someone to call out the names of victims.

This process of posting newspapers in shop windows

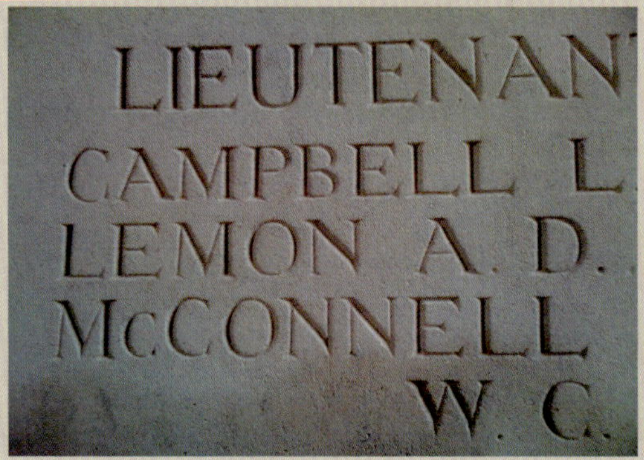

26

26. Archibald Lemon's name is seen here inscribed on the Thiepval Memorial to the missing of the Somme.

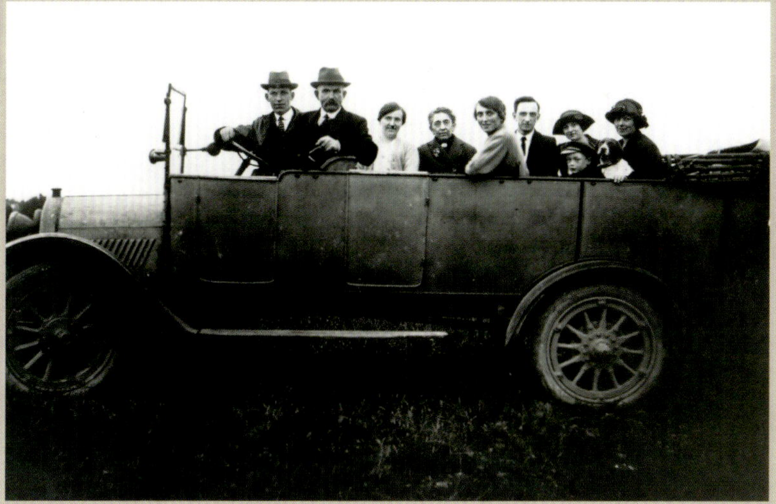
27

was discontinued in the British Isles in March 1917, out of fear that it gave military information to German spies.

Throughout the rest of the summer, memorial services took place in local churches. The *Advertiser* expressed the grief and shock that the community was feeling. The paper noted that from one household

'five young men – McCarthys and Malones – went forth at the call of their country. One of the five was killed on 1st July; two were wounded so seriously that they can serve no more as soldiers; two are now convalescent.'

The paper lamented that 'Hugh Kerr, Francis Kirk Robert Patterson and Patrick Creighton, in years were hardly more than boys' and stressed that 'their names and their sacrifice must not be forgotten.'

Later, details emerged about the injuries experienced by the two Malone boys. One lost the fingers on both hands while the other was completely paralysed.

Many men who were lucky enough to survive, wrote letters home. Corporal James McMaster, who had served with the 15th Royal Irish Rifles, wrote to his shoemaker father in North Street, saying 'I hope I won't see anything like it again...coming back after getting relieved was the worst, for we were doing nothing but tramping over the dead.' And some men arrived home to recuperate from wounds, including Captain Tyndall Johns, an officer in the 12th Royal Irish Rifles who lived in Joymount Place. Johns had been as solicitor in pre-war life, and when the conflict began he had been living at Joymount with an English wife, four children, their governess and a number of servants.

Even as the news from the Somme was sinking in, many aspects of domestic life continued as before. A tennis club continued to meet throughout the summer of 1916 and the local paper declared that 'the art of serving has been properly mastered'. Three-penny tickets were sold for concerts at Sunnylands. Holiday-makers from the city continued to throng Carrickfergus and Whitehead, especially when the sun shone. The local salt-mines were a tourist attraction, decorated with coloured lights for visitors. Horse racing at a track in Clipperstown was a popular spectacle. The *Advertiser* complained about 'the reckless motorists passing through the town', on jaunts along the Antrim Coast Road.

The sight of such joviality perturbed the returned soldiers. Lieutenant James Cordner, speaking in Whitehead Presbyterian Church on a 'Sabbath evening'

27. A charabanc leaves Whitehead for a tour of Islandmagee. Local tourism continued in wartime.

in July, a short distance from the Esplanade, talked about his grim experiences and declared that in light of the war, this was 'no time for anyone to be at ease and planning holidays.'

Some people protested shock in their letters to the paper, not at the casualties on the Western Front but at much more trivial matters. The absence of changing facilities on the Carrick sea-front disturbed one letter-writer. He had witnessed soldiers changing into their swimming gear at the harbour –

'Anyone who is about the East Pier on a warm day can see a squad of soldiers going down to bathe...these soldiers have to divest themselves of their clothing in full view of anyone who cares to look over the wall...'

Another citizen shared this concern, having seen men bathing *'in nature's garb.'*

One correspondent was distressed at hearing the band of the Royal Irish Rifles, marching to church parade each Sunday while playing the secular tune - 'Way down upon the Swanee River' instead of a sacred melody.

Through the rest of 1916, as many Ulster communities came to terms with the cost of 20th century warfare, fresh efforts were made to support the troops. In October, a Red Cross flag day was held in Carrickfergus to help fund this organization which supported prisoners of war. Among the items sold for charity were brooches made from the remains of zeppelins. A branch of the 'Ulster Sphagnum Moss Association' met in the former deanery in Scotch Quarter and planned trips to gather this plant, which possessed soothing, antiseptic qualities. They then created bandages from it, for use in hospitals and nursing homes.

The *Advertiser* reported that 'useful work has been going on in the Technical School where a number of volunteers have been engaged in war work – the making of stretchers, bed-rests, crutches etc....' The newspaper explained that 'anyone who would like to help will be welcome on any evening.'

Each church in the Carrickfergus community attempted to assist men at the front. The choir of the 1st Presbyterian Church sent 'a quantity of comforts' to the soldiers in the 12th Rifles, which had moved to Flanders. The ranks of the Ulster Division were being 'restocked' with conscripts from all across Great Britain. Recruitment in Ireland was drying up, in County Antrim as elsewhere, in response to the Somme losses and because of political challenges posed by the Easter Rising, which had stirred strong separatist sentiments among nationalists.

In the aftermath of battle, survivors from the trenches were making an appearance in the area. Sergeant Hugh Morrison of High Street was recovering from inhaling poison gas. Sergeant David Acheson of Market Place was recovering from 'injuries to the face.' A number of soldiers were looked after at the 'Railway Home' in Whitehead. And the bad news from the front did not stop after the Somme. The paper for 10th November contained the information that 'Private J. Clarke is missing believed killed, in an attack on the 7th October'. He was 'only 19 years of age' and had been 'a clerk in the Northern Bank, Carrickfergus Branch', although coming from Castlerock. The newspaper opined that he had been 'a young man of much promise.'

As Christmas approached, seasonal concerts were held. Men of the Royal Garrison Artillery presented a musical evening at Joymount Presbyterian Church Hall, during which Englishmen in the regiment expressed appreciation of the hospitality shown by local people. Speakers included Bombardier Lindley, who said that 'Joymount was father, mother and home to the men.'

In December, Christmas parcels were sent to the remaining 'Carrick boys' at the front -

'each parcel contains one of Cameron's real good current loaves – "spotted brede" - a tin of oxo cubes, a tin of sardines, a bag of chocolate and another of confectionary, a pair of comfortable woolen socks, a quantity of cigarettes and a plug of tobacco and a card of greeting...'

At Christmas many servicemen obtained home leave and were seen on the streets, greeting old friends and neighbours. There can be no doubt that several local families did not feel like celebrating. One newspaper article, published in December 1916, conveyed the grief felt by the Reilly family, when a memorial service was held for their son Maxwell in Carrickfergus Methodist church.

During the service the parents spoke of their boy.

'... Whether at school or a college or business, Max never caused us one anxious hour and the weekly letter home was never forgotten...'

A missive was read out, written by a padre who had conducted Max's funeral at the front, saying –

'on Sunday afternoon when I called at the hospital, he was delirious, and soon after he passed away. Reverend Gordon and myself laid him to rest in a beautiful military cemetery...'

The service for Maxwell Reilly was concluded when the choir sang the anthem 'Now the labourer's task is o'er' and men of the R.G.A. played 'The Dead March from Saul.'

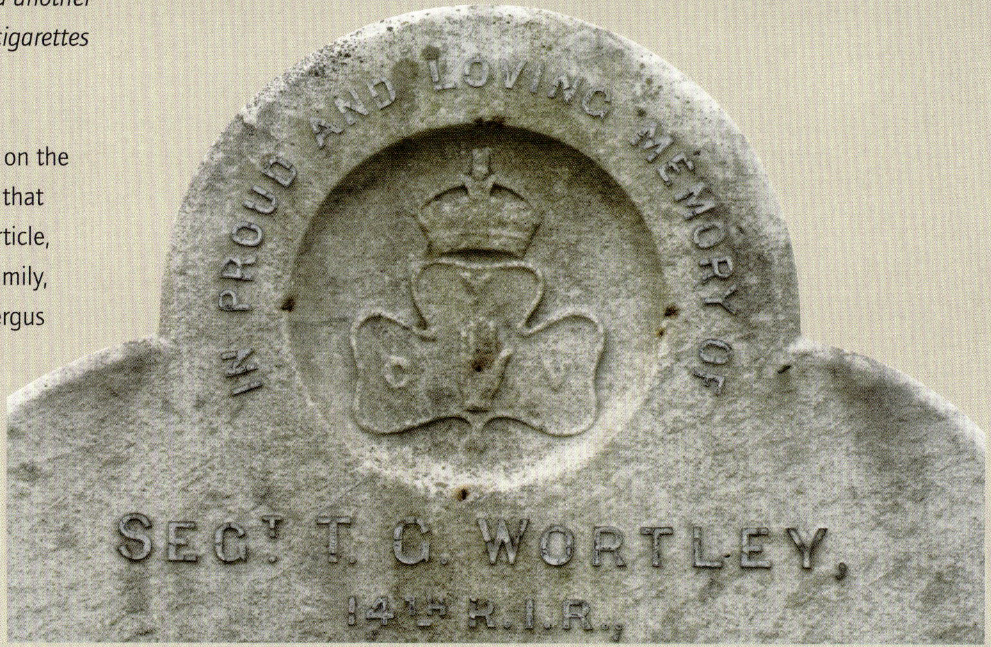

28

28. A commemorative stone in St Nicholas Church of Ireland graveyard for one young soldier who is buried on the Western Front.

1917

The U-boat war against allied shipping proved a frightening threat throughout 1917. Food supplies were endangered and there was a national campaign to create allotments in which citizens should grow vegetables. Carrickfergus Council discussed the issue and some land at Joymount was set aside for the purpose. It was a project subject to problems, when children from poorer parts of town uprooted the plants, either to supplement their own family's resources or out of mere vandalism. Meanwhile, at Whitehead, the golf club had to provide 9 acres of ground for cultivation, under the stipulations of the Defence of the Realm Act.

Shipping in the Irish Sea was vulnerable to submarine attacks and in February the steamer, the *Sallagh*, sailing from Larne to Belfast, was shelled by a U-boat, just off the Antrim Coast. One man was killed and two were injured. The rest of the crew took to the lifeboats, though they were shot at by the Germans, while making for the shore. The survivors were picked up, shocked but unharmed. The men included William Penny from Scotch Quarter and Charles Young from Cheston Street.

As the year went on, other Carrickfergus men were victims of submarine war. Wiliam Clifford of Lancasterian Street became a fatality in the torpedo attack on the hospital ship *SS Donegall*, which took place in April in the English Channel. The *Advertiser* reported that other local seamen had been declared missing. These included Captain James McAlpine and Samuel Hilditch of North Street, James Atkinson of Schomberg Street, W.Carroll of Irish Quarter West, Thomas Dalton of Eden and J.Cameron of Woodburn. James McAlpine had been an experienced mariner, serving his apprenticeship on sailing ships. He left behind a widow, a four year old son and one year old daughter.

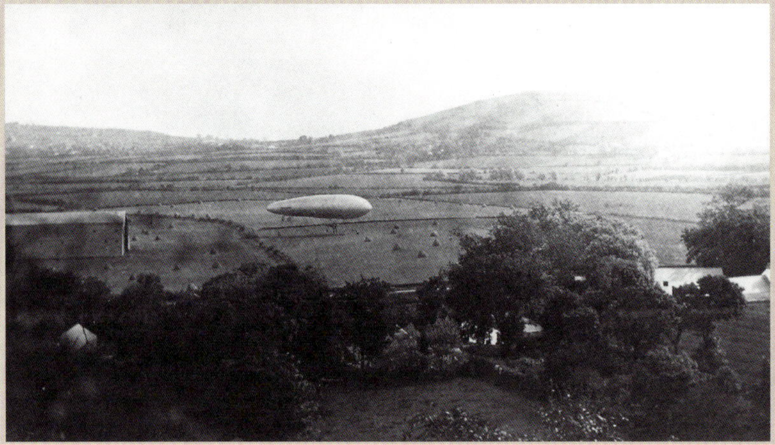
29

The attempt to stop submarines from entering the Irish Sea via the North Channel led to a variety of security measures. These included an ambitious attempt to place an anti-submarine net between Rathlin Island and the Mull of Kintyre and the creation of an airship station near Stranraer, with an Irish sub-station at Bentra, close to Whitehead. These airships were able to spot the periscopes of U-boats from the sky and signal their whereabouts to the Navy. The craft were mainly S.S. class dirigibles, or non-rigid airships, unlike zeppelins, which had metal frames and were larger.

29. Airships, now a key feature of the war against U-boats, were moored at Bentra.

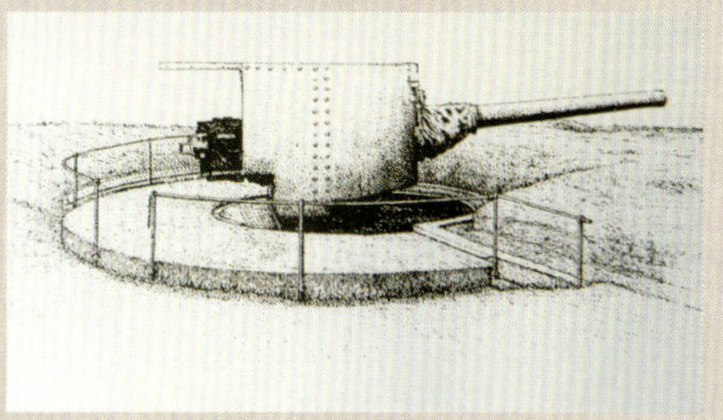
30

The dirigibles were crewed by men of the Royal Naval Air Service. They could climb to more than 5,000 feet, travel at 50 mph and fly for 12 hours at a time. The first S.S. airships were 143 feet long and 28 feet in diameter, containing 60,000 cubic feet of hydrogen, and propelled by a 75 hp Renault engine. The crew of two consisted of a pilot and an observer, who also operated the wireless set. Up to eight small bombs could be carried and a machine-gun.

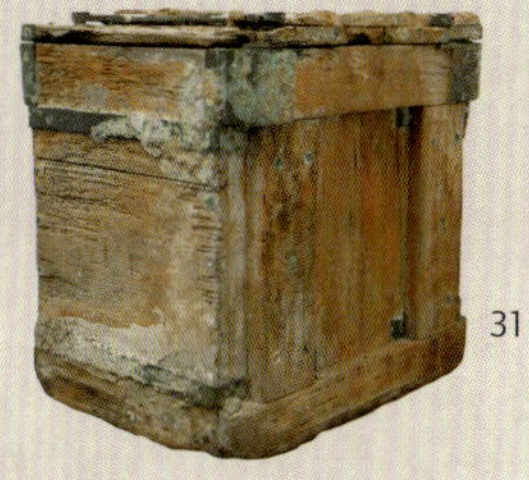
31

In October 1915, an account for Bentra station had been opened in the Northern Bank in Whitehead. Land belonging to a local farmer had been acquired. By 1917, the renewed U-boat campaign was reaching horrific levels, accounting for 1000 allied ships from January to March. This menace had to be combated with fresh vigour. A portable airship shed was erected at Bentra and wooden huts built as accommodation for the staff, which included riggers and mechanics, who looked after the engine, inflated the envelope and repaired damage to the canvas.

The airships engaged in scouting duties, looking out for mines as well as U-boats. Each day a craft accompanied the steamship, the *Princess Maud*, on its journeys between Stranraer and Larne. The ship was often camouflaged with 'dazzle paint' to prevent easy observation by enemy U-boats. The airships performed a crucial surveillance task for the *Princess Maud* as this ship plied a route by which many troops made their way from Ireland towards the war-zone.

By 1917, a more advanced 'S.S. Z' class airship was travelling on the North Channel route, with sturdy frame, 70,000 cubic feet capacity, 75 hp Rolls Royce engine and crew of three. It was an exciting time for locals, watching this airship descend from the sky and seeing the crew disembark, clad in helmets, goggles and heavy coats. Spectators made their way from Carrickfergus, to see one of the key features of the war against the U-boats, which were inflicting such damage on the British economy.

Throughout 1917, ships sank off the Antrim coast and although the *Princess Maud* escaped unscathed, in December the 4,000 ton cargo-boat, *SS Chirripo*, was sunk by a mine, half a mile from the cliffs at Black Head. Built in Belfast, she had been a 'banana boat', operating for the Elders and Fyffe line on the route to the Caribbean, and named after a Costa Rican mountain.

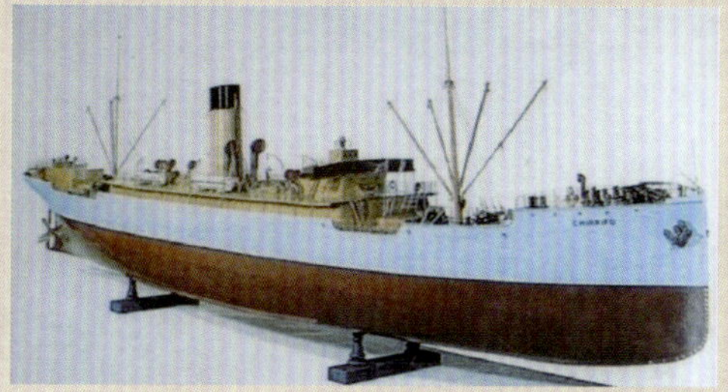
32

Shortly afterwards, *SS Tiberia* was sunk by a torpedo in the same waters, in all probability by the submarine *UB 19*. The armed trawler, the *Rose*, sank off the south Antrim coast during the war years, as did a German U-boat. Decades later, divers would retrieve items from these wrecks, including portholes,

30. The guns at Kilroot Fort continued to fire practice rounds each week but they were of little value against submarines.
31. Ammunition box recovered by divers from *SS Chirippo*, sunk off the coast near Black Head.
32. A model of *SS Chirippo*, sunk by a mine, not far from Black Head.

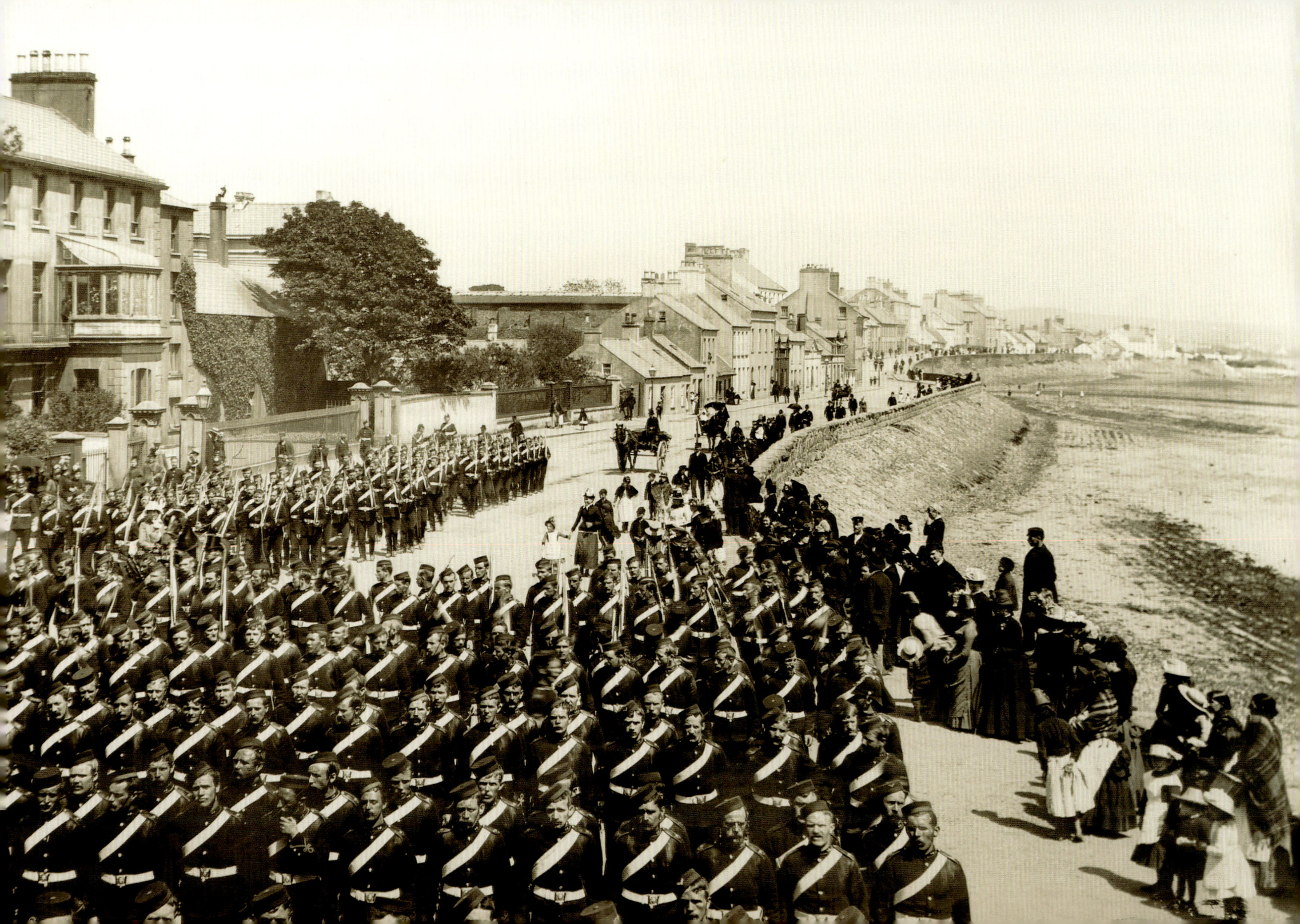

crockery, guns and ammunition. As for the *UB19*, after the war her gun became a trophy and it stands today, across the waters of Belfast Lough, in Ward Park in Bangor.

It is small wonder that paranoia existed along the northern coastline of Belfast Lough during 1917. Nocturnal activities still generated great suspicion, as when the Whiteabbey police were summoned on a summer's night, to 'arrest' two men who had been fishing with aid of a lantern, in a boat a few yards off-shore. They stood accused, by local sleuths, of signaling with their torches to a zeppelin which was about to fly up the lough and bomb Belfast!

The technology of warfare was changing all the time, on the home front as well as in the trenches, where by now tanks, underground mines and poison gas had all been used. Now that submarines and zeppelins could threaten Britain from the air and beneath the waves, the batteries of heavy artillery which had been created to safeguard the British and Irish coastline were less valuable, even though they were of recent build.

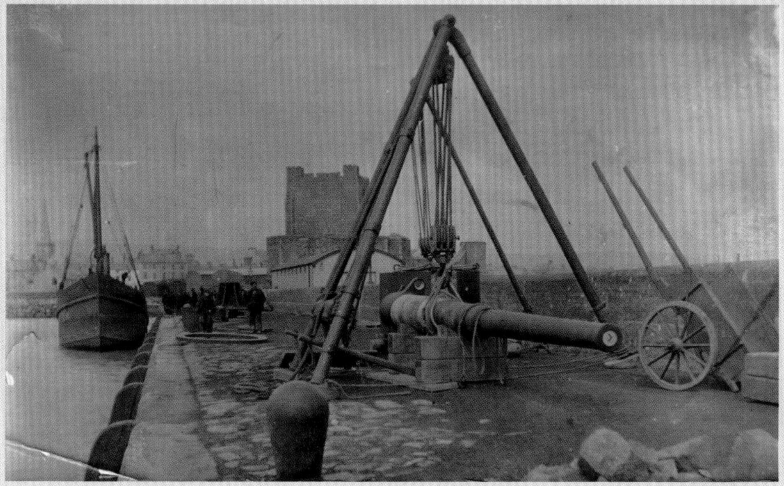
34

The defence of this particular part of the Irish coast had been undertaken by the Antrim Artillery since the mid-19th century, mainly using local men who were eligible for recruitment to the overseas army in time of foreign war. The Carrickfergus locals were well used to bugle-calls each morning and evening outside the 'old courthouse' barracks and the Sunday Church Parade through the streets. Both castle and court house were headquarters for this unit in the latter half of the century, which by 1900 was 1000 strong, although most men at this stage were probably serving in the Boer War.

As the threat of an expanding German navy presented itself in the 20th century, new artillery forts were needed, positioned in less cramped circumstances than a medieval castle and possessing large enough cannon to tackle any unfamiliar shipping which tried to make its way up Belfast Lough, intent on sabotaging shipyards and factories.

As a result, new artillery forts were built between 1907 and 1910, on an older military site at Kilroot in County Antrim, at Greypoint, in County Down coast, and on East Twin Island, close to the mouth of Belfast harbour. A number of 'practice guns' were retained in the vicinity of Carrickfergus Castle.

Now, in the midst of the Great War, the 6-inch Mk VII guns at Kilroot were heard engaging in practice fire every week. The guns were 23 feet long, positioned 100 feet apart on revolving gun carriages and could fire 100lb

33. Antrim artillerymen used to depart for foreign conflicts like the Boer War, as pictured here. Now members of the regiment faced an enemy that lurked in offshore waters.
34. The cannon for the Kilroot Fort had been delivered in 1910 but by 1917, the range and power of the guns on German battleships surpassed that of the coastal artillery.

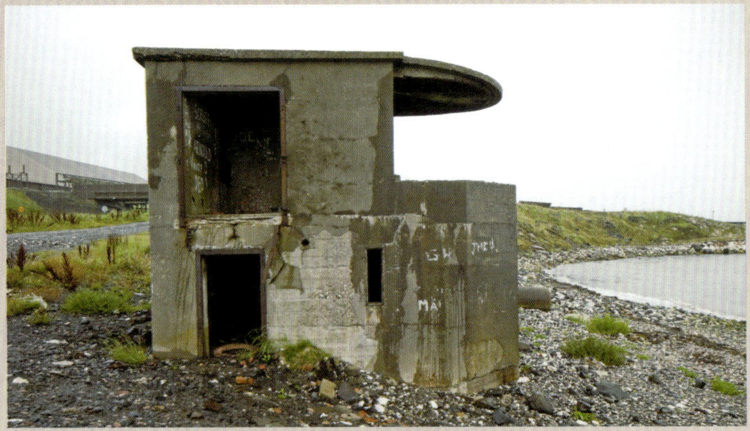
35

shells for 6 miles. They had created excitement amongst local people, when they landed at Carrickfergus harbour in 1911. The gunners were empowered to challenge every vessel that arrived in the lough and to fire on ships that did not declare identity and intentions.

The Kilroot Fort was manned by 40 men through much of the war. They looked after their guns and manned the magazine, stores, command post and a shelter to be used in event of an enemy attack. Operations in an artillery fort required care. Men who entered the magazine where ordnance was stored wore felt-covered boots. Hob-nailed footwear could have created a spark and set off an explosion.

And anyone caught sleeping on duty was given two days in the on-site cells. The troops who guarded the fort were placed in blockhouses, where they manned Maxim machine guns. The entire complex was surrounded by a defensive ditch and barbed wire, to prevent the intrusion of German saboteurs but also, after Easter 1916, to keep at bay attacks by Irish insurgents, keen on seizing military hardware.

The men based at Kilroot included members of the Antrim Artillery, raised primarily in the county, and soldiers from the 15th Company, Royal Garrison Artillery (R.G.A.), recruited across the Irish Sea. They were assisted by men of the Belfast Voluntary Defence Corps.

By 1917, gunners at Kilroot were operating with yesterday's technology. Not only were U-boats and zeppelins fairly invulnerable to artillery but enemy gunboats possessed cannon which could fire over longer distances than the Mark VII. This meant they could sit beyond the range of the Kilroot artillery and lay waste to Carrickfergus and Whitehead. Besides, the Kilroot fort did not possess the technology for searchlights, which meant that during hours of darkness, enemy craft could make their way towards Belfast, if they negotiated the boom which stretched across the mouth of the lough.

An attempt was made to connect Kilroot and Greypoint forts by underwater telegraph cable – divers have subsequently brought to the surface a length of wire which stretched across the lough in the Great War period.

Despite the inadequacy of County Antrim's coastal defence network, men of the artillery were a feature of life in the Carrickfergus area throughout the war, many of them temporarily present in the vicinity before being drafted to the Western Front.

35. Although the Kilroot Fort has largely been demolished deserted artillery look-out posts still stand on the shoreline.

Throughout 1917, some semblance of domestic 'normality' was still maintained. The Carrickfergus rowing club, despite depleted numbers, continued to meet. A 'bathing station' was established near the pier, including changing facilities. The Carrick Glee Singers gave several concerts, with the ticket money sent to a Blinded Soldiers' and Sailors' Home in London. Horse Racing took place at Clipperstown in June. Carrick Dancing Class met in the Good Templar Hall, a building which belonged to a well-known international temperance organization, dedicated to tackling the scourge of alcohol abuse.

The *Advertiser* continued to lament the 'reckless motorists driving though the town', as they went on weekend outings along the coast.

The huge battles of Messines and Ypres, which were fought in the Belgian region of Flanders, continued to suck in Ulster soldiers, including those who still fought with the 36th Division. In August the *Advertiser* reported the funeral of one man with Carrickfergus origins who had been wounded in a recent battle and sent to a hospital in England. Hugh McDowell had been wounded in the right cheek, while serving with the 7th battalion, Canadian Railway Troops.

The injury seemed a mild one but dirt in the wound had caused problems and a bone infection called osteomyelitis set in. Infection spread to his respiratory system and moved to his brain, ultimately resulting in death. Medical records reveal that his demise was slow and unpleasant. Wounded on 1st of August, he took two weeks to die. He felt 'pain and numbness of legs with loss of power' and his speech became slow. Soon he developed 'loss of control of bladder and rectum' and then widespread 'paralytic symptoms.' He finally expired on 15th August at 8am.

The local paper reported on his interment, which took place in Ireland rather than Canada –

' The funeral of the late lance-Corporal Hugh McDowell took place on last Friday afternoon to St. Nicholas churchyard...the remains had been brought over from England on the previous night and the funeral left Carrickfergus railway station at 3 o'clock. An escort and firing party of the Royal Irish Rifles accompanied the remains, which were placed on a gun carriage, the coffin being covered in a Union Jack. The Reverend Alexander Cuthbert MA, minister of the 1st Presbyterian Church, officiated at the graveside and paid high tribute to the memory of the deceased, who had been intimately associated with the YMCA and church work in Carrickfergus and was a candidate for the ministry in Canada. The firing party then gave the usual salute of three volleys and the last post was sounded, which brought the sad occasion to a conclusion...'

For the Dalton family of Lower Woodburn there was no corpse to inter in a local churchyard, as their son Bobbie, with the Royal Irish Rifles, had died of wounds during the Battle of Messines. The parents received a letter from Nurse McPherson which indicated that he had been buried in Belgium. The writer sought to console the family that despite his severe 'gunshot wound of the chest', he had 'kept continually speaking of his mother' and

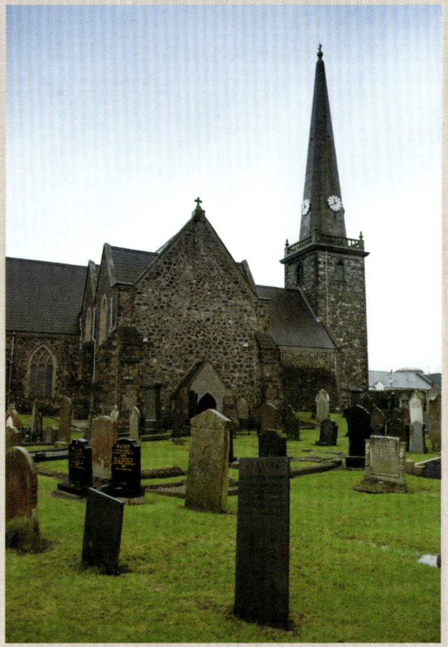

36

36. St. Nicholas Church, Carrickfergus.

saying that 'she was not to worry about him'. The nurse enclosed a lock of Bobbie's hair.

For the citizens of Whitehead, news throughout 1917 was also bleak. On 14th March, the submarine *U44* attacked *SS Bray Head*, commanded by Captain John Hoy who came from the town. Shelled by the enemy, *SS Bray Head* went down in the Atlantic, 580 miles from the Irish coast. Captain Hoy's lifeboat, which he shared with members of his crew, was never seen again.

Meanwhile in Captain Hoy's home town, care was being given to soldiers' children who had arrived there from Belfast. A holiday home in Edward Road had been in operation since 1915, with a remit for the children of servicemen. As Christmas 1917 approached, festivities were arranged for boys and girls who had a father at the front and a mother who was incapable of looking after the children, through illness or extreme poverty. In their holiday home

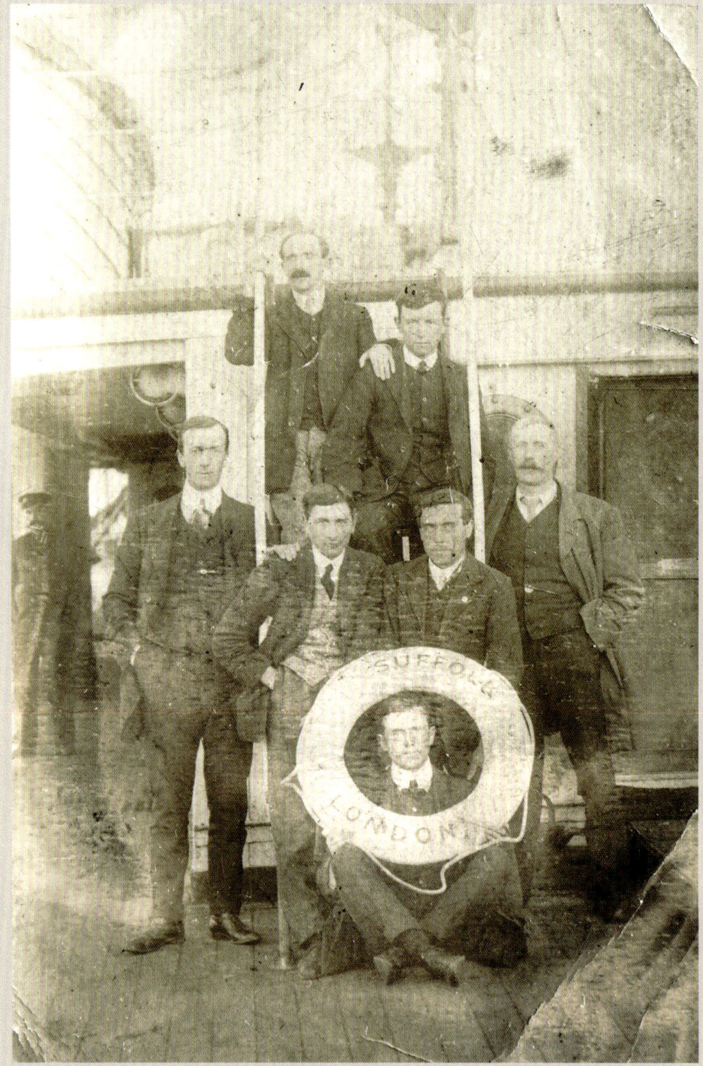

37

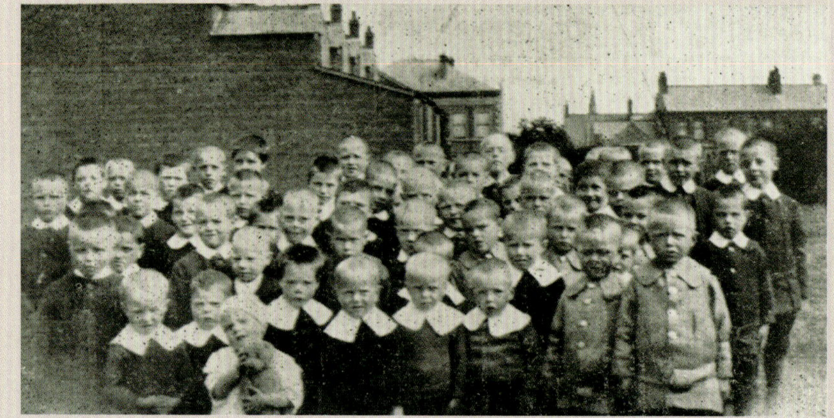

38

37. Captain John Hoy is seen here with fellow-mariners. He was lost at sea, 580 miles west of the Irish coast.
38. Children of servicemen being cared for at Christmas-time in a holiday home in Whitehead.

the children were given a sense of Yuletide magic, with the aid of a 'Christmas tree with its fairy lights and gifts' which was a source of 'wonder and delight'.

As 1917 drew to a close, there were changes at Sunnylands camp in Carrickfergus. The 4th Royal Irish Rifles were replaced at Sunnylands by men of the Royal Fusiliers, from England. From his pulpit, the rector of St. Nicholas offered the new 'guests' a hearty welcome.

Less welcome in many peoples' eyes, was the labour dispute that affected the life of the harbour in November. The men who handled the coal went on strike, demanding 2d per ton increase in wages, to bring them into line with remuneration offered at Larne and in Belfast. The dispute was swiftly settled but it was a reminder that not everyone expected to make sacrifices for the war-effort if that meant they had to endure economic injustice.

And it was crystal clear that not everyone in the vicinity was enduring privation or trying to live with patriotic frugality. The pages of the *Advertiser* throughout 1917 featured a range of luxury goods, on sale at various premises in the town. A new shop belonging to a Mr Parks was opened in Market Place in 1917, selling a range of 'high-class millinery' and a 'fine range' of other 'up-to-date goods.' Another local shopkeeper, J.G.Cameron, seems to have had no trouble selling his confectionary, pastries and home-made jellies for 'soirees, socials, excursions and picnic parties'. W.M.Vint's business continued to thrive, baking 'Bride and Christening cakes' and other specialities.

Indeed wartime in Carrick was clearly a period of some culinary experimentation. By 1917, the *Advertiser* carried regular articles about wholesome, affordable 'nice dishes', which the housewife might be inspired to try, including 'stewed vegetable marrow....duchess potatoes.... and blackberry pudding.'

Some local businesses were experiencing commercial success. Butterfield's Motor and Cycle Agency moved during 1917 from its cramped West Street premises to a more commodious location in North Street. A few local businessmen were astute enough to sense a market for wartime goods. By 1917, Cambridge and Co. were advertising a 'Harrison's Pomade' which was gauranteed to 'kill all insects on hair and body' and would make the ideal present for a loved one who was suffering from the vermin that always plagued British soldiers in the trenches.

The same firm was happy to sell increased supplies of 'super-phosphate, bone compound, barley manure and basic slag' which were in greater demand than ever as tillage increased, and farmers did their duty with regard to the food shortage.

Local construction and home maintenance work did not entirely falter during the war years. Gorman's saw-mills and slate-yard continued to do a brisk trade in 1917, selling 'bright spruce deals, genuine Bangor Blue slates and fire clay goods.' The McCartney Brothers also maintained a successful painting and decorating business in Joymount.

However, once again a wartime Christmas came and went - the fourth festive season since conflict began. Seasonal good cheer could not mask the sense of disquiet and fear. Many of the citizens of Carrickfergus and Whitehead wondered when the conflict would come to an end.

1918

The new year brought little comfort. There was much talk of introducing conscription to Ireland, in order to bring it into line with practice in the rest of Britain. Many unionist leaders and Protestant clerics supported such a move but it was never implemented. In the wake of the Easter Rising, Ireland was deemed to be too volatile.

And the submarine threat had not gone away. A government order in early February restricted the light shown in buildings within 5 miles of the Irish coast between sunrise and sunset. For the first time, this placed Carrickfergus, Whitehead and most of the rural hinterland in virtual blackout during the long hours of darkness. Wartime conditions now seemed to be getting worse. Weekly prayer-meetings, pleading with God for victory, were held in Carrick YMCA each Friday evening.

Carrickfergus citizens became aware of the suffering of other nations during this global conflict. Charity collections were made for the Armenians who, in the 20th century's first act of genocide, were being displaced and slaughtered by the Turks. Displays of Armenian needlework went on sale at various venues.

News from the front in March was not encouraging. The Germans made a breakthrough, pushing British troops back for several miles and capturing many prisoners, including soldiers from the Ulster Division. Meanwhile, at home, military training went on. Flares were seen in the sky over Sunnylands, as troops practised night-time manoeuvres and the echoes of grenades were heard from the Orlands estate, where bombing practice was undertaken. The sound of the Sunnylands bugler, playing Reveille in the morning and the Last Post in the evening was still heard each day throughout the town, as was the call of the bugler outside the courthouse. At Bentra, small aircraft were now using the airfield as well as airships.

Accidents did occur during training, as the *Advertiser* reported in early May

– 'A distressing fatality occurred on Monday at Orlands, at bombing practice...Lt. Stewart stumbled and fell and a grenade, which was attached to the end of a rifle he was carrying, was knocked from its clip and exploded...(and he) died within half an hour of the incident.'

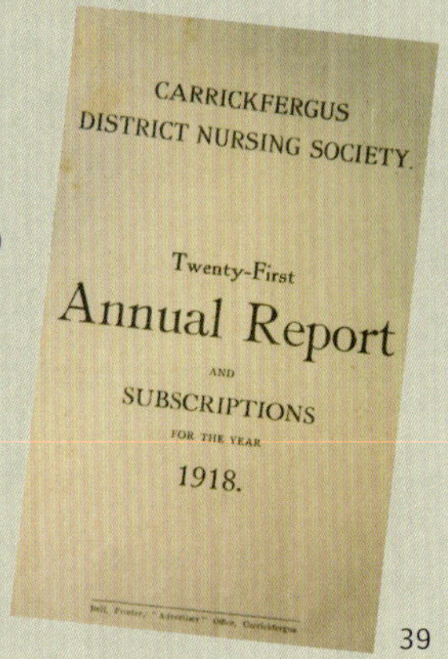

39

To deepen the gloom, in June the first cases of a strain of influenza were reported in the area. The 'Spanish Flu' was a worldwide epidemic. It struck down the young and healthy in particular.

In this final year of war, local citizens continued to engage in 'normal' civic life and holiday-makers tried to enjoy themselves. Charabancs took tourists from Whitehead Railway Station on tours of the coastal scenery. A pierrot troupe performed yet again on the Esplanade. A new drama society was formed in Carrickfergus. The Kilroot annual ploughing match went head.

39. Local nursing in 1918 was preoccupied with care for the victims of the highly infectious 'Spanish Flu'.

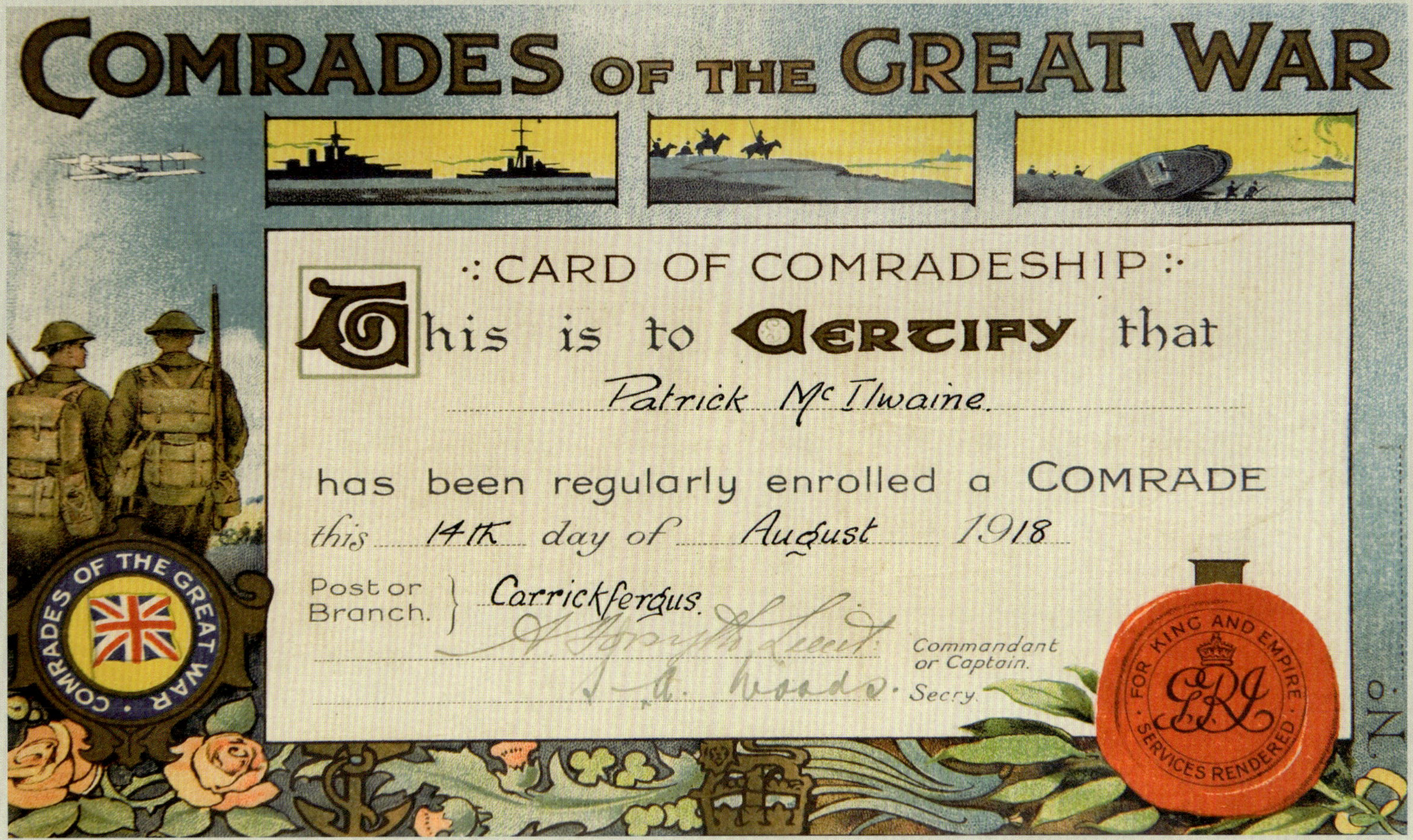

40

40. The nationwide organisation known as Comrades of the Great War offered local solace to many returned servicemen.

The band of the Royal Fusiliers played concerts at Shaftesbury Park and in the Garden Battery, in the shadow of the Castle. An organization for veterans of the conflict, called 'Comrades of the Great War', held its first meetings in the courthouse.

Then as summer turned to autumn, better news arrived from France. The German advance had run out of steam. The tide had turned for the British and French, newly aided by American soldiers. The allies were soon sweeping all before them. In Germany, the fabric of society was crumbling, as food supplies diminished and industrial unrest grew. The possibility of German surrender began to look more likely.

Then on 11th November came the information that everyone had been waiting for since 1914. The Western Front fell silent at 11am. The Germans had agreed to an armistice and thereby accepted defeat. The Great War was over, having resulted in millions of casualties and having changed the lives of those who had lived through it.

In Carrickfergus, on 11th November , pent-up emotions were released.

' The boys of the 6th Royal Fusiliers who received the welcome concession of a holiday, marched through the town, headed by the regimental band. [The crowds were] singing and cheering and waving flags and the church bells joyfully announced the great event and the horns, whistles and sirens of the various public works in and around the town and on the steamers in the harbour were sounded, flags were flown from almost every house in the town, the old church tower and the North Gate were bedecked, the vessels in the harbour all hoisted their colours....When darkness fell, bonfires were set ablaze in various parts of the town. A torchlight procession marched through the principal streets and an effigy of the German monster was consigned to the flames...'

The local newspaper described how 'groups of excited people congregated everywhere', many watching the fireworks above Sunnylands camp. The local authorities had taken the precaution of ordering the closure of public houses in the evening, in case celebrations got out of hand. Thanksgiving Services were held in churches. In church halls 'tea and amusement' was provided.

However celebrations were dampened by the effects of Spanish Flu –

' Many homes have been desolated by the ravages of influenza. There is scarcely a street where there are not several families mourning the loss of loved ones. Sergeant Weston of the Royal Fusiliers sorrows in the loss of his wife and only child. Mr Samuel Lyle Beattie of Fairymount has lost his wife, infant son and sister-in-law.'

But despite such sorrows throughout the remaining weeks of 1918, familiar patterns of life re-emerged. Blackout was no longer needed. Ships proceeded to sea with all lights burning and navigation lights were restored in the lough. The airships left Bentra for the last time. The boom of coastal artillery ceased. Military manoeuvres ended at Sunnylands and Orlands.

A General Election, held on 14th December, showed signs of a new order in Ireland. While the Unionist candidate, Lt Colonel McCalmont, was a

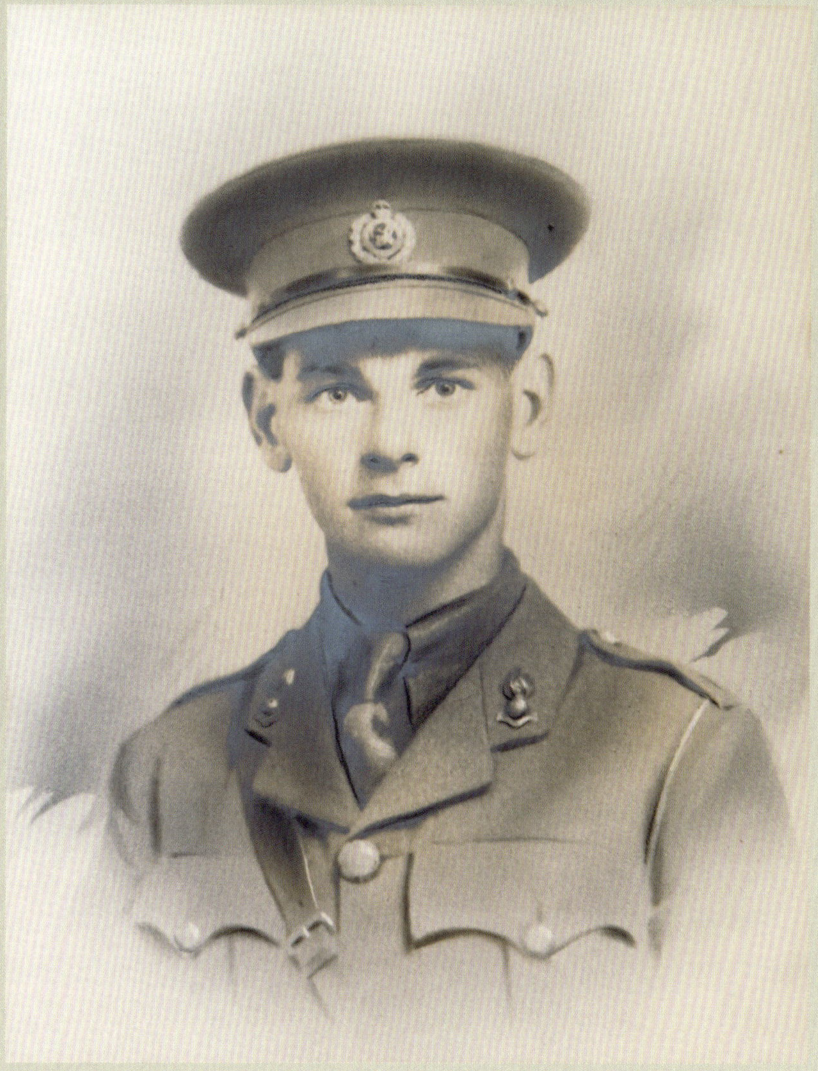

41

clear winner in the East Antrim constituency, the presence at the hustings of Daniel Dumigan of Sinn Fein was an indication of things to come in Ireland. Dumigan only secured 5% of the vote and there is no evidence that he received any great backing from nationalist voters in Carrickfergus or Greenisland. However Sinn Fein was a militantly separatist party which, in the wake of the Easter Rising, had begun to gain the loyalty of a majority of nationalist voters on the island of Ireland.

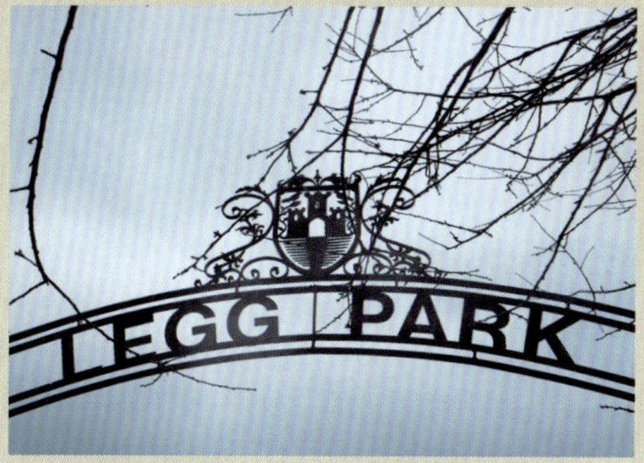

42

The country was heading down the road towards civil strife and eventual partition.

As this narrative has demonstrated, some towns in Ireland were very militarised places throughout the war years. Barracks towns and maritime communities were particularly affected. The unionists who dominated in Carrickfergus and Whitehead could accept such militarisation as confirmation of their Britishness but many barracks towns and harbours in Ireland were in deeply nationalist areas. The intense, militarized and sometimes crisis-ridden Great War atmosphere can only have helped make the case for the revolutionary analysis of Sinn Fein in barrack towns and ports with a much stronger nationalist tradition, such as Limerick or Dundalk.

The social legacy of four years of combat was a profound one in places such as Carrickfergus and Whitehead. Many 36th Division veterans would not return home till after Christmas but there was sufficient demobilisation in December for the *Advertiser* to take note that –

41. Tragic news continued to unfold as war came to an end. Charles Legg died in the last few weeks of the conflict.
42. One Carrickfergus landmark which denotes an individual Great War tragedy.

'the Carrick lads are returning slowly...R.Milliken, J.McAtamney, R.Hamilton, H.Simms, A.Caters. D.Atkinson, H.McAteer, J.Weatherup...'

Men like these were often traumatised and they would struggle to adapt and integrate within the post- war era, although local clubs and organizations to which they once belonged soon resumed activities, having had their wartime existence curtailed by the presence of many members in the forces. Not least of these clubs was Carrick Rugby Club, which had watched many of its young players leave for the front.

The Orange Order in and around Carrickfergus had lost ten men on the battlefield. Two had also been lost at sea and four endured the experience of being a prisoner of war. Lodges in the area mourned the death of much-loved brethren. Richard McMaw had been a member of Lodge No. 1544, known as the Kilroot True Blues. He had been 26 when he died at the naval Battle of Jutland, in 1916.

Some local families did not find out the nature of their sufferings until after the armistice. The *Advertiser* reported on 20th December that 'Mrs McDowell of McKeen's Row has received news that her second son, Rifleman Thomas McDowell, 12th RIR, died of influenza on 22 October, at Minden POW camp. [He was] taken prisoner on 1st July 1916 [and was] a former blacksmith's helper at the International Salt Company Ltd...'
1918 had also seen the death of John O'Donnell, a machine-gunner with the Royal Irish Fusiliers. He left behind a grief-stricken wife, two children and his aging parents, who resided on the Islandmagee Road, close to Whitehead.

At Christmas, there were painful reminders for many families of the men who had not returned home. Thoughts were also turning to public memorialisation. In light of the losses sustained by the 11th and 12th Royal Irish Rifles – the South Antrim and Mid Antrim Volunteers – thought was now being given to a memorial for the men of the county. Sites such as the Giant's Causeway and Cavehill were suggested. One other suggestion was for a monument on Knockagh heights, overlooking the lough.

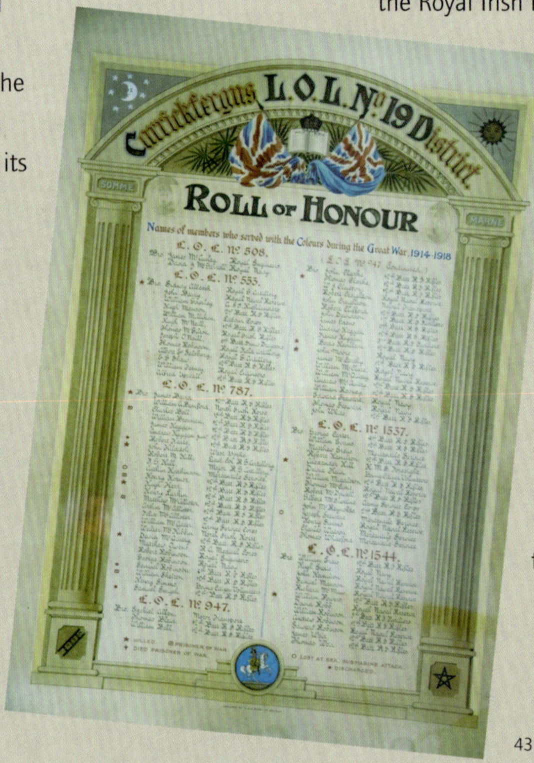

43

43. A Great War Roll of Honour hangs in the Orange Hall in Albert Sreeet, Carrickfergus.

Postscript

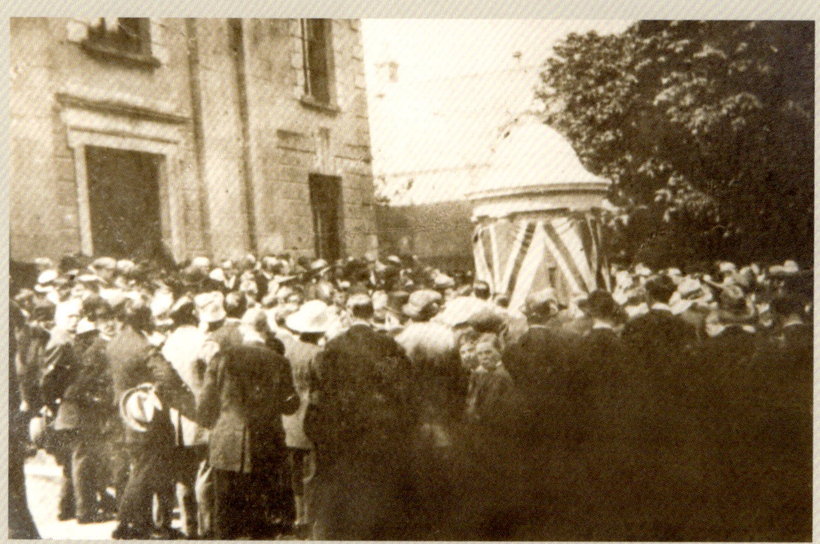

44

The County Antrim monument would take time to move from conception to completion. However, activity began straight away in several local churches to create memorials to the dead. By the end of 1919, building work was underway on a campanile in St. Nicholas churchyard, called the 'Heroes' Tower', containing a peal of eight bells. The North Street Presbyterian Church began building a cenotaph in the church grounds. At Joymount Presbyterian Church, there were thoughts of dedicating a pipe organ to the memory of the fallen and the Congregational Church had similar ideas. The Methodists hoped to dedicate a pulpit to men who had given all for their community.

Plaques containing the names of those who had perished were placed on church walls and in workplace locations during the post-war years. The plaque at Whitehead Presbyterian Church contained the names of 57 men and women who had served, including six who had perished.

Many civic institutions created rolls of honour, including the local branches of the Loyal Orders. In Barn Mills, a memorial was established, containing the names of all those who had gone to die at the front. In the offices of Carrickfergus Salt Union, a plaque in memory of former employee, William Skelton, was erected.

Bereaved individuals held on to memorabilia that spoke of the life of a much-loved relative. Thomas McMullan's sister, Isabella, who had looked after her young brother on the demise of their mother, was particularly saddened by his death from Spanish Flu while still in the ranks. She kept a picture of Thomas in uniform, his regimental badge and a brooch that he had brought her from Canada. Isabella's grandchildren still possess these items as well as Thomas's army knife and fork.

In the *Advertiser*, families who lost loved ones at the Somme placed notices in the 'In Memoriam' column each July. Other families chose relevant wartime anniversaries. The widow of Arthur Hodkinson of Eden placed a notice each November, in memory of her husband who was lost at sea when the *SS Garron*

44. A crowd gathers to take part in the opening ceremony for the war memorial outside the Presbyterian Church in North Street.

Head was torpedoed on 16th November 1917. The grandmother and aunts of James Kyles, killed in action with the 2nd Royal Inniskilling Fusiliers, inserted a notice, which concluded with a prayer for their dead boy –

'...on whose soul Sweet Jesus have mercy.'

July 1919, despite being the anniversary of the Somme deaths, was also a time for celebration as the Paris peace conference came to a close with the signing of the Treaty of Versailles. People thronged the streets of Carrickfergus and Whitehead and fireworks displays took place. Prayers of thanksgiving were offered and hope was expressed from many pulpits that a more peaceful era had come at last.

By the 1920s, the process of creating graveyards for the men who died on foreign battlefields had begun. Local names appeared on wooden crosses and eventually on more permanent gravestones in locations as diverse as Gallipoli and Flanders.

For those who died at sea, there was no known grave.

In graveyards in south-east Antrim, gravestones were erected for men who perished from wounds and illnesses contracted in the course of duty or in other local calamities. One stone in the churchyard of St. Nicholas Church of Ireland pays tribute to T.G Wortley. The memorial is inscribed with the crown and shamrock of the Young Citizen Volunteers, the elite UVF unit to which he had been proud to belong, before joining the army. In the tiny, tree-lined Catholic cemetery to the rear of St Nicholas Catholic Church may be found the grave of Father Henry, mentor to so many Great War troops.

Major W.H.Davey of the Northumberland Fusiliers was laid to rest under a simple gravestone in Victoria cemetery. Within days of the armistice he returned home to take part in the General Election, as a pro-Home Rule candidate for the Irish Parliamentary Party, standing in Duncairn, against the unionist candidate, Sir Edward Carson. Returning to peacetime duties with the army in Europe, he had contracted 'blood poisoning' and this had done irreparable damage to his health. On 29th August 1920, he died at his home in Bawnmore Road in Belfast, leaving behind a widow and young family.

On the day of Davey's funeral the cortege passed swiftly through Belfast on account of 'the disturbed state of the city'. Blinds were drawn in houses along the route of the hearse through Carrickfergus, on its way to the cemetery. Presbyterian clergymen officiated. The coffin was draped in a Union Jack. A cap, sword and belt were placed on top, along with a laurel wreath which possessed the inscription – 'To darling Daddy from Mammy, Dermod and Baby Pat'.

By 1921, the process of collating a list of the local Great War dead had been undertaken. 17 names were known to the authorities in Whitehead. They included many well-known local people, such as J.L Walker, who had run a fine bakery in the town. Local churches in the seaside town compiled their own lists of those who had taken part in the war.

In Carrickfergus, lists of the fallen were compiled. Estimates arrived at over 130 names. As with all lists of wartime dead, it was hard to know who to

45. J.L. Walker with his staff, standing outside his Whitehead bakery in more peaceful times. He did not return from the war.

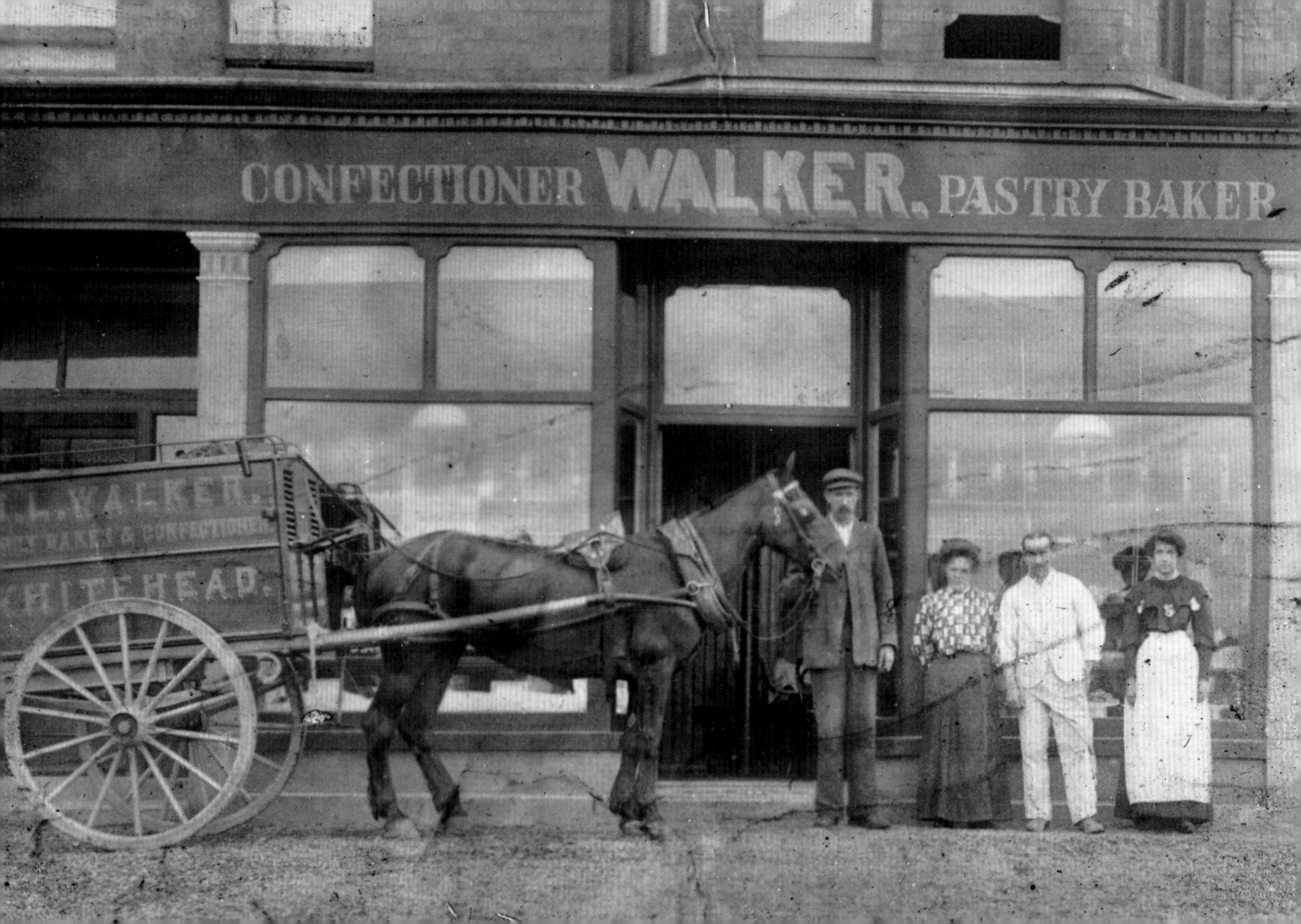
CONFECTIONER WALKER. PASTRY BAKER

include. Should Whitehead men be included? Should Carrickfergus men be mentioned who had emigrated in the pre-war era, only to join the forces during the conflict? Should Ballycarry men be noted, who joined up with their Carrickfergus friends and served in the same platoon? What about men from Greenisland? Was W.H. Davey a casualty of war or of peace? Should Gunner Ruddy be named, even though he died in a self-inflicted local accident? What about merchant seamen who had drowned?

Louis MacNeice's father also drew up a list of men who had served in the war and survived, as opposed to those who had perished. The number of 520 is striking. We do not know if this list refers only to men from the town of Carrickfergus, whether it includes the town's wider hinterland or names of all the emigrant soldiers. Nor do we yet know how many of the men whom he listed saw active service on the battlefield or naval engagement as opposed to domestic duties. The list also appears to leave out those who served as merchant seamen, whose ships were often torpedoed by U-boats.

However, if the figure of 520 applies to the town of Carrickfergus alone, and to that list is added the approximate figure of 130 war-dead, then this small town - with a population of less than 5,000 – manifested a rate of involvement in the war which is very striking.

On 11th November 1921, three years after the armistice, services of remembrance included a two minute silence and the refrains of Last Post and Reveille, sounded by a bugler from the castle walls. Wreaths were laid at the Heroes' Tower and the cenotaph in the Presbyterian church grounds in North Street. In October 1922, the foundation stone of the County Antrim memorial

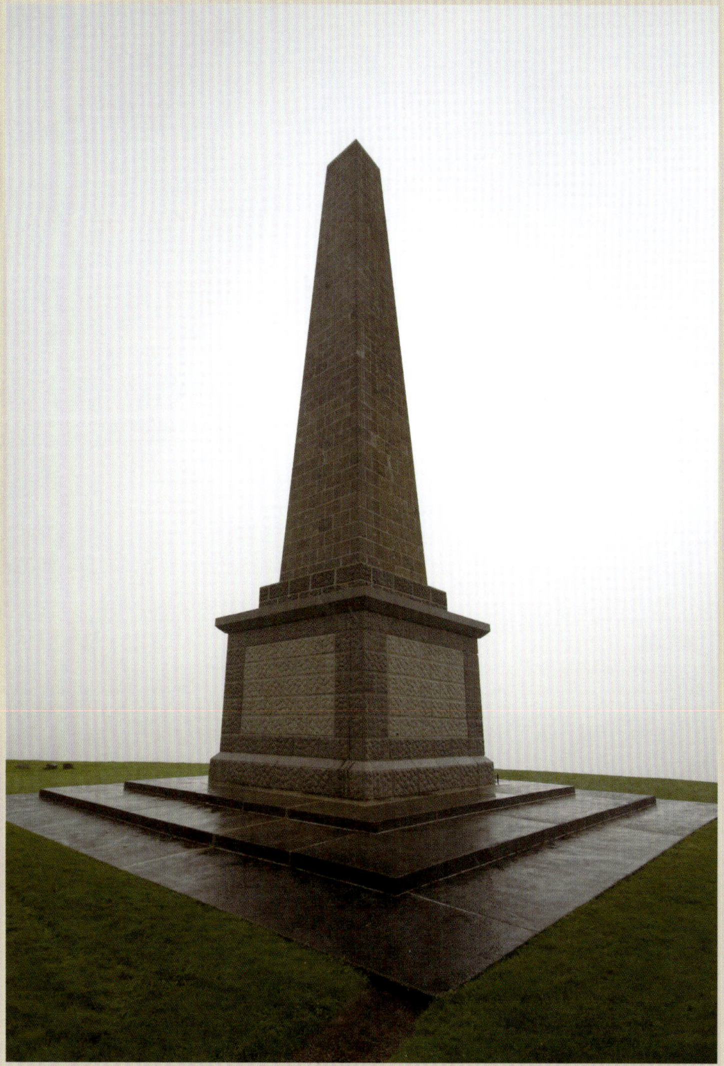
46

46. The Knockagh memorial to the war-dead of County Antrim, which overlooks Belfast Lough.

at Knockagh was laid. The proposed guest-of-honour was Field Marshall Sir Henry Wilson but he had been assassinated in June, during the fierce War of Independence which had emerged from the brewing civil conflict in Ireland, at the end of the Great War.

Throughout the post-war decades, the process of remembrance developed and by the mid-1930s, the Knockagh Memorial was completed, after a struggle with finance. In France, the Thiepval Memorial to the Missing of the Somme was finally erected, containing the names of some of the Carrickfergus troops in No 6 platoon, within B company of 12th Royal Irish Rifles. Their bodies had never been retrieved from the battlefield, after the tragic attempt to capture the Railway Sap, on the banks of the Ancre.

In the late 1930s it was clear that an era of peace had not dawned at Versailles. The words of the rector of St Nicholas at the Somme memorial service in July 1921 had been perceptive. the *Advertiser* noted his observation that once again – '...unless there was great watchfulness, they might be asked to give their boys of 15 to 20 years of age for a war that need never come... such a war was quite possible'.

The rector went on to say that people should 'tell their politicians that the time had come for settling the disputes between nations without resorting to either strikes or wars – by conference, conciliation, settlement by arbitration...' Such methods were not effective with Adolf Hitler. Before long, men and women of Carrickfergus and Whitehead would be called to make more sacrifices, as war against Germany resumed. Troops from the United States of America and Belgium would be based in Sunnylands and other local barracks.

Hundreds of soldiers, airmen and sailors would walk the streets, the Antrim Artillery would be resurrected and a deadly submarine war would once more rage in Atlantic waters. The Germans would indeed bomb Belfast from the air, though no longer utilizing zeppelins.

A new set of names would soon be written on local war memorials,

It was not until the 1960s that plans were made to give Carrickfergus a civic cenotaph and to provide Whitehead with a shared memorial. The unveiling of the latter monument occurred in 1969, just as Ulster was being launched into a new phase of civic disturbance.

Changes in the monumental landscape of Carrickfergus had occurred by this stage. The cenotaph outside the North Street Church was replaced with a war memorial hall. The Heroes' Tower was demolished in 1959 due to structural problems which made it unsafe – even though the town's bell-ringing fraternity recalls that the demolition experts had difficulty knocking it down! A bell tower above the gateway was opened in 1962 and contained the peal of bells from the old structure. The practice of ringing these bells each 1st July morning continued until comparatively recent times.

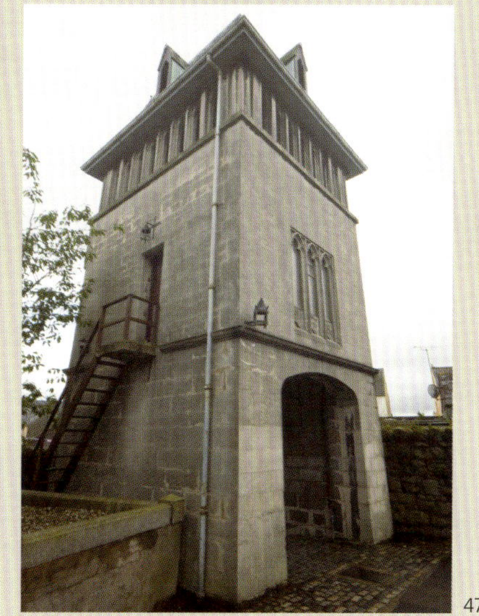
47

47. The War Memorial at the entrance to St Nicholas Church of Ireland is both a gateway and a bell-tower.

One enduring memorial to the Great War is Legg Park, situated close to the Model Primary School in the town. The Legg family bequeathed money for the establishment of this civic amenity in memory of their son Charles, who had been a lieutenant with a field company of the Royal Engineers. He died eight weeks before the Armistice in an accident at a casualty clearing station in France.

Many years after the armistice, some veterans were alive and well. Barney Murtagh, who had come to the town from Cavan with the Royal Irish Fusliers, returned to his Carrickfergus wife, settled down and opened a barber's shop. He walked with a limp - a legacy of a wartime injury. His son Terry recalls that there wasn't a day when Barney did not treat his family to wartime reminiscences. He was fond of stories about boxing exploits. In 1955, Barney gave up full-time work and passed the business on to Terry. He died in 1980.

Other old soldiers came to live in Carrick. George Lindsay spent his final years in the town. He had been a County Derry man and as a cycling enthusiast had joined the cyclists' company of the Ulster Division. During one spell of leave, George had a difficult visit to make, to console the family of his pal, Robbie McCauley, who had been one of the Barn Mills volunteers –

' I came to tell Mac's mother of his death in 1917. Mac was only 17 and my friend. She'd quite a family round her when I visited, four or five maybe. "Well, Mrs McAuley" I said "You'll not be left alone." "But" she said "my Robbie was the flower of the flock" That's the way it seemed to be. All the best chaps seemed to be taken.'

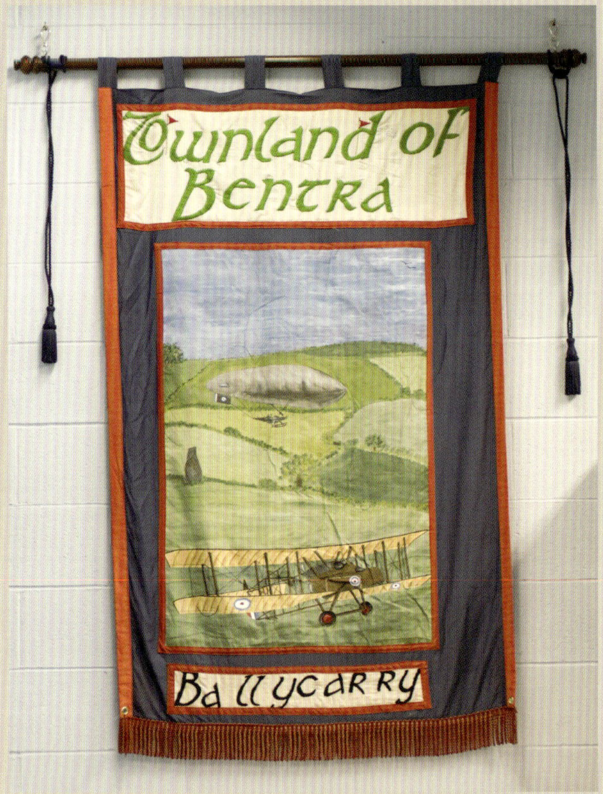

48

48. The 'Bentra banner', which commemorates the years when airships and aeroplanes used a base in the townland.

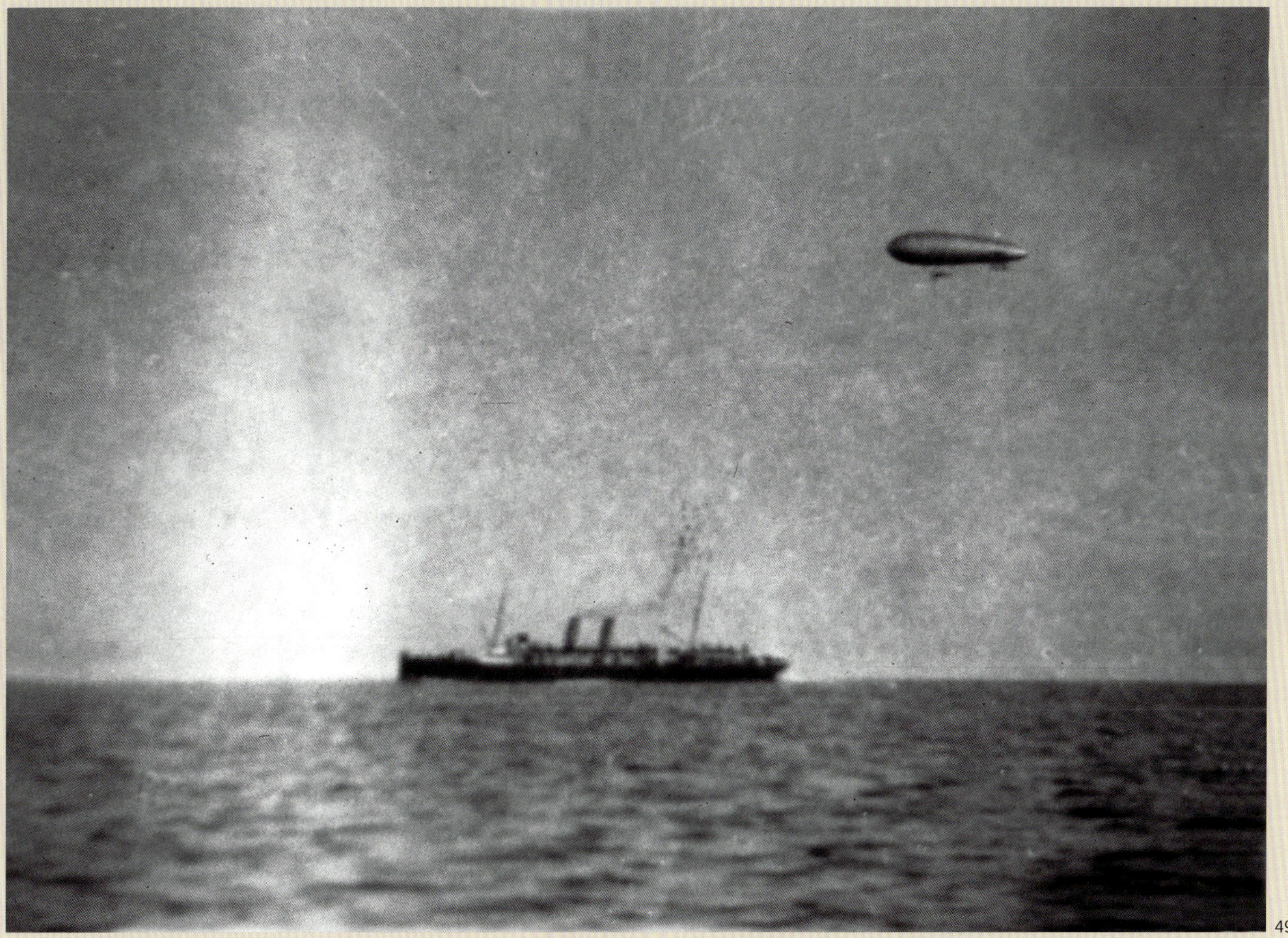

49

49. Protected from the U-boat threat by an airship escort, *SS Maud* makes its way across the Irish Sea to Scotland.

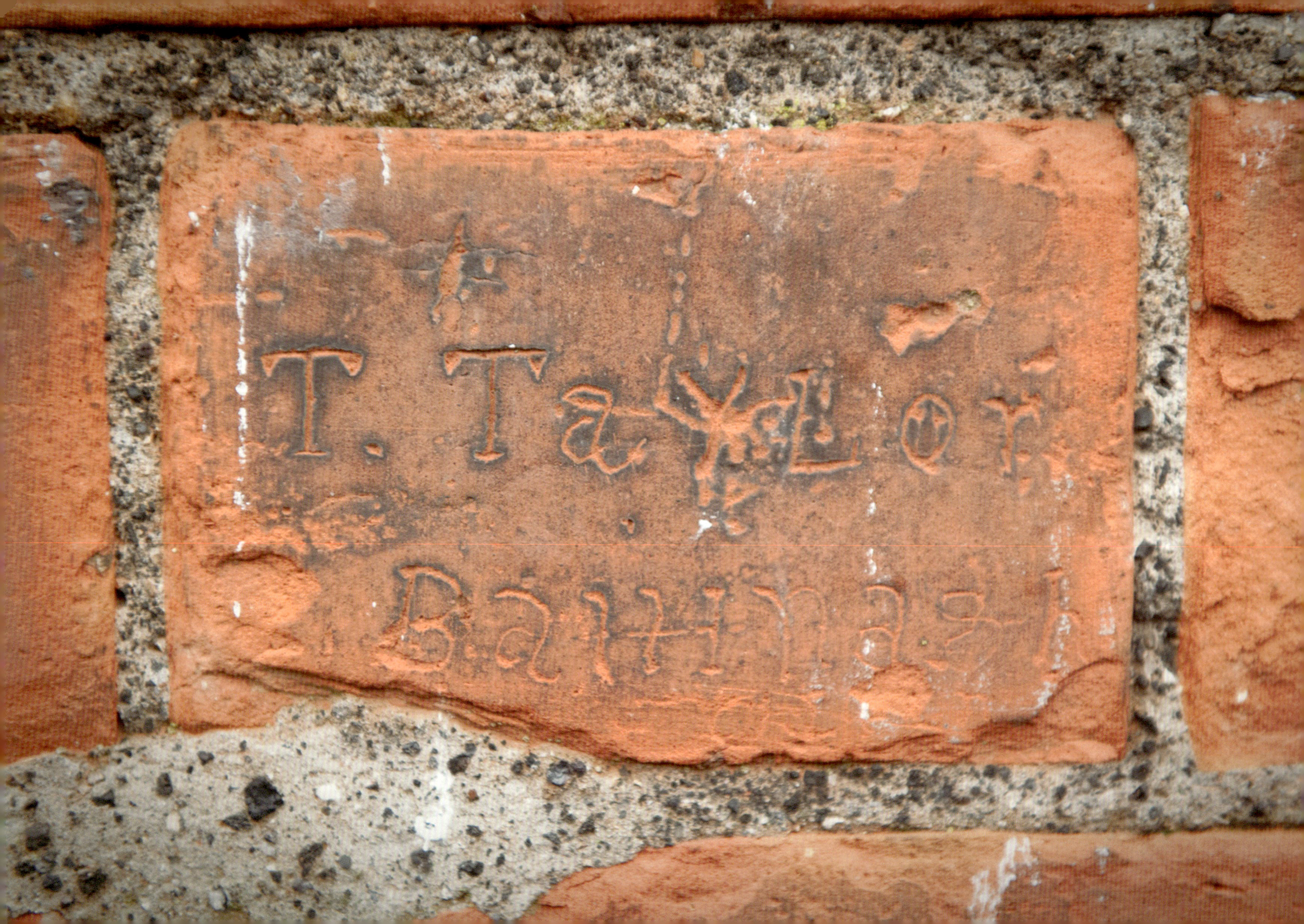
T. TaYLor

George lived to be over a hundred years of age, in all probability the last voice from the war in the Borough of Carrickfergus. George's story points up the fact that not everyone who came through the Great War was permanently traumatised or had their lives foreshortened. One local veteran, Walter Brownlee, came through the conflict unscathed and went on to father fourteen children!

Recent attempts have been made by local communities to ensure that the era is not forgotten. In Ballycarry community centre, there is a banner celebrating the role of the Bentra townland in 20th century history, through a portrayal of its wartime airship and aeroplane base. Guy Warner has written a book on the Great War aeronautical heritage of south-east Antrim. In Whitehead Library, a painting by Stephen O'Donoghue gives imagination to the idea that ghosts of local men who died in wartime still return to the public memorial where they are commemorated.

Meanwhile, at Kilroot, the gaunt and lonely remains of the Great War artillery battery are still seen, despite the fact that Royal Engineers in the Territorial Army subsequently demolished most of the fort while practising their use of high explosives.

And on the walls of the former ordnance stores in Carrickfergus may be found graffiti created by men from the Great War era and the pre-war years. Etched into the red-brick surface are the names of soldiers from as far afield as Ballina in County Mayo and Dundalk in County Louth.

The local desire to pay respect to men who died in this conflict still exists today. The British Legion has discovered the burial spot where Hugh McDowell was interred within St. Nicholas graveyard in 1917. Having consulted parish records the Legion now knows where this hitherto unmarked grave exists. There are plans for erecting a gravestone to commemorate this forgotten soldier, who had been born in Carrickfergus, joined a Canadian regiment and died in a hospital in England.

Perhaps the most well-known testimony to those far-off years in Carrickfergus is offered by the poet Louis MacNeice, who, as a small boy, lived in the St. Nicholas rectory, before moving to boarding school in England. His is a very different poem from the ones penned by unsophisticated local soldiers during the conflict.

A poem is of course a literary artefact rather than an historical account but it nonetheless conveys an intense flavour of the wartime town where MacNeice grew up. Then in 1917, he left for Dorset, crossing the submarine–infested North Channel on board the *Princess Maud*, accompanied by his father and step-mother.

During those Carrickfergus years he had been mourning the death of his mother, listening to his father preach each Sunday and observing the sights, sounds and smells of a town where poverty and privilege co-existed. When the war broke out, he had watched young soldiers await the call to the front, marching away from Sunnylands Camp to the places where death and injury loomed. Several years later, as one of Ireland's finest writers, he could still recall the atmosphere of war-time life on the northern shores of Belfast Lough.

50. Men from all across Ireland left their names etched upon the walls of the Carrickfergus ordnance stores.

CARRICKFERGUS

I was born in Belfast between the mountains and the gantries
To the hooting of lost sirens and the clang of trams
Thence to smoky Carrick in County Antrim
Where the bottle-neck harbour collects the mud which jams

The little boats beneath the Norman castle,
The pier shining with lumps of crystal salt;
The Scotch Quarter was a line of residential houses,
But the Irish Quarter was a slum for the blind and halt.

The brook ran yellow from the factory stinking of chlorine,
The yarn-mill called its funeral cry at noon,
Our lights looked over the lough to the lights of Bangor
Under the peacock aura of a drowning moon.

The Norman walled this town against the country
To stop his ears to the yelping of the slave
And built a church in the form of a cross but denoting
The list of Christ in the angle of the nave.

I was the rector's son, born to the Anglican order,
Banned forever from the candles of the Irish poor;
The Chichesters knelt in marble at the end of the transept
With ruffs about their necks, their portion sure.

The war came and a huge camp of soldiers
Grew from the ground in sight of our house with long
Dummies hanging from gibbets for bayonet practice
And the sentry's challenge echoing all day long;

A Yorkshire terrier ran in and out by the gate-lodge
Banned to civilians, yapping as if taking affront:
Marching at ease and singing 'Who killed Cock Robin?'
The troops went out of the gate lodge and off to the Front.

The steamer was camouflaged that took me to England –
Sweat and khaki on the Carlisle train;
I thought that the war would last for ever and sugar
Always be rationed and that never again

Would the weekly papers not have photos of sandbags
And my governess not make bandages of moss
And people not have maps above the fireplace
With flags on pins moving across and across –

Across the hawthorn hedge the noise of bugles,
Flares across the night,
Somewhere on the lough was a prison ship for Germans,
A cage across their sight.

I went to school in Dorset, the world of parents
Contracted into a puppet world of sons,
Far from the mill-girls, the smell of porter, the salt-mines,
And the soldiers with their guns.

Louis MacNeice (1907-1963)

Acknowledgements

The author wishes to acknowledge the contribution to this project made by many people. In particular, Paddy O'Donnell, Guy Warner, Doreen Corcoran and Graham Walton gave permission for several photographic images which are in their possession to be published in this volume. They also permitted me to draw on expert research which they themselves have carried out.

The expert enthusiasm of many other people proved invaluable, helping me to accumulate and interpret a range of relevant artefacts, documents and images. Thanks to William Blair and Jayne Clarke of the Mid-Antrim Museums Service. Thanks is also due to David Fitzpatrick, Amanda Moreno, Terence Murtagh, Helen Rankin, Des Blackadder, Denis Gough, Peter Stevenson, Jack Aiken, Irene Walder, Stephen Johnston, Sean McIntyre, George McFall, the family of Walter Brownlee, the family of George Lindsay, Ballycarry Community Association, members of Ulster's diving fraternity, members of Whitehead Presbyterian Church, local members of the Orange Order, staff at the N.I. Environment and Heritage Service and members of the local branches of the Royal British Legion.

Carrickfergus by Louis McNeice is reproduced by permission of David Higham Associates, London.

Ordinance Survey map reproduced with the permission of Landed Property Services under delegated authority from the Controller of Her Majesty's Stationery Office.
Permit No 100022.
2010

Carrickfergus Museum & Civic Centre,
Antrim Street, Carrickfergus BT38 7DG
www.mid-antrimmuseums.org

This book has received financial support from the Northern Ireland Community Relations Council which aims to promote a pluralist society and encourage an acceptance and an understanding of cultural diversity.

Views expressed in this book do not necessarily reflect those of the Community Relations Council.